Changing Water Into Wine:
The Gospels in Rhyme

Joseph Muller, Poet
Sean Cleary, Artist

Published by

Seattle   Charleston

CreateSpace
Published by CreateSpeace, Charleston, SC

LIBRARY CATALOGING DATA
Muller, Joseph
Cleary, Sean
Changing Water into Wine: The Gospels in Rhyme/Joseph Muller; art by Sean Cleary
226.05209
ISBN-13: 978-1514743058

ISBN-10: 1514743051

Printed in the United States of America
July 2015
First Edition

Joseph would like to thank…

my parents, Mary Anne and Arthur Muller, grandparents, Daniel and Anne Marshall, and Marie Muller, aunts, uncles, nieces, nephews, and other relatives who taught him the faith early on, and showed me what Christian love is. I'd like to thank my siblings, Anne Rebecca, Danny, and Mary Kate, for their lifelong friendship, support, and inspiration. I'd like to thank Fr. Coman Brady, Fr. Raymond Dundon, Fr. Vincent O'Connell, Fr. Fred Marano, Fr. Joseph Calise, and many others who have shown me that the good done by the Church is a hundred times greater than its flaws. I'd like to thank my friends for all the companionship and humor they have brought to my life, especially Marty O'Shea, Laura Brennan, and Liz Keohane. I'd like to thank all my teachers, who helped me learn this stuff and inspired me to be an educator, and all my students, who have made it a career choice which never bores. I'd like to thank Sean Cleary, for the incredible beauty he has added to my poetry. Finally, I'd like to thank my wife, Jennifer, and kids, Sean and Keira, who have made marriage and fatherhood as rewarding as I could have ever imagined.

And I'd like to thank God for the wonderful source material. And for everything else.

Turning Water Into Wine: The Gospels in Rhyme

Table of Contents

[6]

[8]

Chapter IX: Jesus at the Feast of Tabernacles in Jerusalem............page 234

Chapter X: The Ministry in Judea..page 256

[11]

* Unlike all of the other passages, which were close translations of Gospel passages into rhyme, the appendix is a piece based purely on my imagination/theological speculation, which uses Scripture and the Creed only as a starting point.

Introduction

I have been asked countless times how I got the idea to write this work, why an epic poem and why one based on the Gospels. Actually, I got the idea for this when I was in high school, when the things I most enjoyed to read were from Chaucer, Dante, and other epic poets. I thought how sad it was that all of the great epic poets were ancient or medieval, and when they were Christian, they were so full of references to ancient mythology that modern readers, myself included, miss a great deal of them. I first thought that a saint's life would make the ideal Christian epic, but found most lack the great conflict readers expect. Then I realized I was missing the most obvious Christian epic, "the greatest story ever told".

The Gospels have converted a third of the world to Jesus' radical message of love and, when actually followed, have inspired countless people to live for others and to be people of charity and peace. People like to blame religion for wars, as if greed and power are not the actual motivations, and as if humanity was far more peaceful before Christianity and more peaceful since Christianity has lost the popularity it once had. If one looks more closely, however, we can see that basically every single positive social movement, including abolition, women's rights, the anti-war movement, the civil rights movement, the pro-life movement, labor unions, the environmentalist movement, (I'll even include prohibition in case there's anyone reading this whom I haven't alienated yet), etc., has been inspired by the Bible. So if I can bring people to the Bible, who knows what the result of that could one day be?

With this hope, I started to write this as a senior in high school. I wrote a few passages, retelling the Temptation in the Desert and parts of the Sermon on the Mount, and some of it was pretty good. However, I wrote one couplet that made me stop the project entirely. Translating Jesus going away for some solitude after John the Baptist was executed, I wrote, "He went in a lake, He went in a boat/He went for His sake, for John He did dote." Though I was probably very sleep-deprived at the time, there is just no excuse for writing that bad. The line was so distasteful that I thought if anyone was to take up the project of rhyming Scripture, it should not be me. Or at least not before I have a lot more practice at poetry. (My humility has its limits.)

About six years later, I was blessed with brief unemployment, followed by a job at a bank without customers. Not entirely without them, but few enough to work on poetry in between customers. I set myself a goal of 50 lines per week, 10 lines each day. I was unable to write even that much for a long time, but eventually, I was able to compose more than double this, and within two years, had about 6,000 lines.

The simple words of the Gospels have a timeless organic beauty. While my initial thought was to add my own commentary (a style that shows up a little in the Infancy Narratives), I soon changed my approach, and tried to simply enliven the wisdom and beauty of the Evangelists' words. I made accuracy my highest priority, blending conflicting stories rather than choosing one over the other, whenever possible. Occasionally, I added a metaphor or explanation, usually when a rhyme could not be found from the text. Of course, my own slant does show in some of these, even revealing the time of my life when it was done. For example, I began to write this when my wife was finishing her first trimester of pregnancy, and I think I referenced Jn. 16:21 (when Jesus compares his Passion to childbirth) about three times in the epic. Other favorite passages, like Mt. 25:31-46, got referenced in similar teachings, and current world events even caused me to add Rom. 12:20ff to the Sermon on the Mount. ("Love your enemy…" is enhanced with "If your enemy is hungry, feed him…")

So in harmonizing the four, I tried to preserve and combine, possibly even enhance, the following:

Mark's Gospel has traditionally been seen as greatly inferior to the other three, standing out for what it lacks from Matthew and Luke. This was until it became almost universally accepted that Mark was the first written, and that Matthew and Luke copied a great deal of their material from him. Then, any unfavorable comparisons sound like comparing the special effects of The Wizard of Oz to a Star Wars movie. Now we realize that Matthew and Luke were standing on the shoulders of a giant. And while this alone did not make me fall in love with Mark's Gospel, reading *Say to this Mountain* showed me how incredibly prophetic and counter-cultural his Gospel is.

Matthew's Jesus has such amazing speeches, like the Sermon on the Mount and the speech condemning scribes and Pharisees towards the end of it (Mt. 23:1-36). As a teacher, you just have to love how Matthew lays out the faith for the reader, and some of his unique parables, like the Final Judgment, are unparalleled. It is so beautiful and so fearsome simultaneously: I want a God who demands that we be charitable, but I fear I don't meet the criteria.

Luke is so intent on showing the importance of forgiveness, love for the poor, women, the marginalized, etc., that people almost forget how central these are in the other three Gospels as well. And he is such a great storyteller, one could hardly imagine Christianity without the Prodigal Son, the Good Samaritan, the Rich Fool, and the Lost Sheep. While some just have one straightforward meaning, the rich symbolism of others can be dissected revealing layers and layers of meaning. One can see in the Prodigal Son not just an exceedingly forgiving God, but an older brother who is self-righteous and judgmental, who sees his relationship with his father as one of slavery (the Law) rather than a loving community, and who cannot accept any forgiveness of a brother. In the Good Samaritan, we see not just a lack of charity, but an almost comically preposterous priority of ritual law over laws of charity and in the Rich Fool, it shows not just the pointlessness of greed, but how socially isolating selfishness is.

John's Gospel, to me, is like really sweet candy. In small amounts, I think "What a beautiful reflection on the mystery of Christ." In large doses, I wonder why this guy can't stop talking about Himself! Broken up, I think the reader has a great chance to enjoy the meditations, but with Synoptic stories interwoven with it. I would place a few of his passages together, to get people in the meditative mindset of John, but then moved back to the other three before that became too much.

When many theologians make their main focus the authors of the Gospels, more than Christ Himself, they miss the forest for the trees. I believe what Raymond Brown wrote, that, for all their best efforts, the most historically accurate picture of Jesus would come from simply reading the four canonical Gospels. So I did my best to include every detail possible, and leave out things only when I had a very good reason.

In terms of what is missing from the canonical Gospels, I left out John 1:29-34, in which Peter and Andrew become apostles, because the synoptic Gospels tell a very different and more famous version of the same story ("I will make you fishers of men."). Also, when Jesus later asks, "Who do you say that I am?"(Mt. 16), Peter says He is "the Messiah, the Son of God", to which Jesus responds that human tongue has not told him this. The John story, however, has Peter told that Jesus is the Messiah in the very first chapter, so I left that out of my version.

The genealogy ("Abraham begot Isaac, Isaac begot Jacob…") also had to be left out because, besides that many modern readers skip over this part anyway when reading the Gospels, it would be just about impossible to rhyme, not to mention the choice of either choosing between Mt. and Lk. or doing two versions of the section. And there were a few details in Luke's infancy narratives which do not match historical records, in addition to the difficulty of rhyming "Emperor Augustus" and "Quirinius, governor of Syria" with anything. Luke's prologue (Lk. 1:1-4) and some of the closing lines in John's Gospel (Jn. 20:30-31, 21:24-25) were also left out because they are words specifically from one writer to their specific audience, and did not make sense to translate into a harmonization. I guess that's about it in terms of major changes. You'll notice that within the text, when I took the artistic license to add or change a small detail, I tried to footnote it to avoid the confusion of "Did Jesus really say that?", assuming this is the closest many people will come to reading the four Gospels.

As I wrote this, I took great efforts to footnote anything a reader might need to know about the passage. Some are simple things like which Old Testament chapter and verse is being referenced, or that a metaphor I've used is an addition to the original text. Others might be more interesting, like why I decided to name the unnamed daughter of Jairus Colleen, or the cultural knowledge which is essential to understand "turn the other cheek". In order to fit the art without shrinking the text, I had to move these to the end of the book, but I strongly urge reading them.

I mentioned in the first paragraph how a big story wants big conflict, and I think many who have done the Gospel story have felt the desire to add to the Jesus-Satan conflict. My initial approach of a looser translation had me consider inserting the devil into the background, not unlike "The Passion of the Christ". I soon realized, however, that I had to be as literal as possible to give the text the respect/reverence it deserves and to make it a work of Scripture rather than my twist on Scripture. (I say that in terms of what I wanted, not to criticize "The Passion", which is in many ways a great film.) I came up with the idea of an appendix which would expand on the "He descended to the dead" tradition both as a way of getting a more dramatic battle between good and evil, and a way to use a bit of imagination in a work that otherwise takes all its ideas from other writers.

Having said all that, I hope I haven't bored you with all of the technical details, but I know any project of this nature can be dissected for its accuracy. Whether this is your first time reading the Gospels, or they are something you have read many times, I hope this shows the truth and beauty of the Gospels as you have never seen them before.

[17]

Chapter I
The Infancy Narratives

1 The Prologue
Jn. 1:1-18

In the beginning of all was the Word,
And through Him all creation has occurred.

The Word was always with God and the Word was God.
In Him was life, which lit the way that good men trod.

Now shining in the darkness is this light,
Which could not fall to dark, abysmal night.

A man named John was sent here from on high,
Not to illuminate, but testify,

Preparing people to the Word of God receive,
That all mankind might in the Word, the light, believe.

The true light, which enlightens all came down to earth,
Although the world knew not His Father nor His worth.

For only through Him was the world created,
Yet by His Chosen People He was hated.

But as for those who gave Him welcome and believed,
The power to be children of God they received,

Those born not from men's blood, nor men's desire,
Nor from the will of man, but one much higher.

In truth, the Word became flesh, dwelling here,
And in our midst in glory did appear,

The glory from His Father, as His only Son,
So filled with grace and truth that His cups overrun.[1]

John witnessed, "This is He of whom I said,
'He who comes after me has passed ahead,

Since long before my birth this one existed.'"
With countless gifts has mankind been assisted.

Through Moses, Yahweh's prophet, God gave us His law,
While Jesus gave such truth and grace we were in awe.

To all except the Son is God concealed,
Who, being near God's heart, made Him revealed.

2 The Birth of John the Baptist is Foretold
Lk. 1:5-25

In days when Herod was Judea's king,
Though under Rome in almost everything,

A priest there was, whose name was Zechariah,
Whose son would pave the way for our Messiah.

He and Elizabeth, his lovely bride,
Could not conceive, although they long had tried.

This lonely couple was in years advanced;
Their righteousness could hardly be enhanced.

Now, while he served as priest, when 'twas his turn,
They chose, by lots, that he would incense burn

In Yahweh's temple, as crowds outside prayed.
But, suddenly, he found himself afraid.

For, on the altar, lo!, an angel stood,
Whose aim Zechariah misunderstood.

The angel said, "My friend, please do not fear.
As sure as you can talk, the Lord can hear.[2]

In nine months hence, your wife will give birth to a boy.
You'll name him John, and both of you will know such joy,

And many will rejoice over his birth.
His fame will spread, in time, o'er all the earth!

He shall be great before the Lord, Divine.
He shall consume no strong drink and no wine.

This world, made dark by sin, he will illume,
Filled with the Spirit, even from the womb.

He will help turn Israel's sons back to the Lord
And fathers' hearts to their children will be restored.

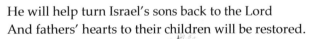

In the spirit and power of Elijah,
He will precede the Lord, son of Abijah.[3]

The disobedient he'll help make wise,
By urging they repent and he baptize.

So they might have the sense of the upright,
Preparing people to be in God's sight."

"How can I know this? Can you show a sign?
We can't! We're both as old as Palatine!"[4]

"For, Gabriel I am, sent for this news,
By God, to pave the way to save the Jews.

Since you would not believe God's holy word,
And thought a prayer answered by God absurd,

I'll prove it genuine, all you have heard:
You shall not speak till all these things occurred."

The crowds outside thought something might be wrong,
Since Zechariah stayed in there so long.

He tried explaining, but his voice was mum,
And they knew that a vision made him dumb.

After his week at Temple, home he went
And they conceived a baby, heaven-sent.

Elizabeth, for five months, kept this hidden,
While giving thanks that her shame had been ridden.[5]

3 The Annunciation
Lk. 1:26-38

When six months pregnant was Elizabeth,
The angel then appeared in Nazareth

To Mary, a most beautiful[6] young maid,
Who, having seen this angel, was afraid.

The angel said, "Rejoice and celebrate!"
And, yet, his looks still did intimidate.

 "Fear not! The Lord's good favor you have found.
The Lord is with you, much more tightly bound

Than you could think. His child will you bear,
The answer I foretold to Daniel's prayer.[7]

You'll name him Jesus, His name will be great:
'Son of the Most High,' they will designate.

The Lord, your God, will give him David's throne;
The house of Jacob, like a king, He'll own.

Throughout all of eternity His reign will span."
"How can that come to pass, since I have not known man?"

 (She was betrothed to Joseph, not yet married,
And knew not how a child could be carried.)

"Think not a miracle cannot come true.
The Spirit of the Lord will come to you.

The power of the Lord, the God Most High,
Will overshadow you, like at Sinai. [8]

They'll call him Son of God, and undefiled,
He'll always be, just like a newborn child.

And, since I speak of children, truth be told,
Elizabeth conceived, though thought too old!

For nothing by the Lord cannot be done."
"I am God's servant, I will bear His Son."

4 Mary Visits Elizabeth
Lk. 1:39-56

Since she knew what was meant by agape,[9]
She heard the news and quickly went away,

Leaving her home behind, in Galilee,
To help her cousin through her pregnancy.

Once she arrived in Zechariah's home,
As soon as hearing Mary shout, "Shalom!",[10]

The infant in Elizabeth's womb leapt.
Filled with the Spirit and with joy, she wept,

"Above all other women, you are blessed,
For holy is the offspring of your nest.

I stand here overwhelmed! How can it be,
The mother of my Lord should visit me?

Behold, for once your greeting reached my ear,
My infant leapt, the sense of which is clear.

For you shall see, that much will be extolled
The one who trusts in what the Lord foretold."

"My soul proclaims God's glory with elation,
Rejoicing in the God who brings salvation,

For He has seen His humble servant's shame
And given me such undeserved acclaim.

All generations hence will call me blest,
At least by those by whom the Lord's professed.

His name is holy and His love unending.
His arm has made the arrogant descending.

He's pulled down princes and the lowly risen,
Cast down the wicked, freed the just from prison.[11]

Unto the poor, He's given them their fill,
The wealthy, they are sent away with nil.

For Israel, He has come to her aid,
Fulfilling promises that He has made,

Of mercy, charity, and faithful love,
For all His people, here and up above."

5 The Birth of John the Baptist
Lk. 1:66-80

When neighbors heard she gave birth to a boy,
The whole community shared in their joy,

All shouting out, "How gracious is the Lord!" [12]
For now her dignity had been restored.

They had him circumcised on the eighth day,
But what he would be called no one could say.

Their relatives thought he should take the father's name,
But it instead would God's benevolence proclaim.

Elizabeth insisted, "Call him John!"
Yet, still this name was not agreed upon.

"But no one in your family bears that name,"
They said, and thought the father thought the same.

The father asked for something to write on,
And showed agreement: "My son's name is John."

And after writing this, he spoke it, too,
Which made the gathered bellow, "Sacre bleu!"[13]

The rumors spread throughout Judean land
Of miracles that few could understand,

At least in full, though all knew it good news.
"Who is this child? Might he save the Jews?"

For, in their hearts, this joyful news was stored.
"This boy must be in the hand of the Lord!"

[26]

6 The Canticle of Zechariah
Lk. 1:67-80

Filled with the Spirit, one cannot its words deny.
Before all those gathered, now he would prophesy. [14]

 "How blessed is our God, who visits us,
Who long has promised help, so help He does.

He freed His people out of slavery,
Rewarding faithfulness and bravery.

He raised a saving horn from David's house.
He would do all for Israel, His spouse,

As through the ancient prophets He proclaimed,
He would not let His bride ever be maimed

By those who hate us, by our enemies,
Just as was promised in antiquities

In covenants given to Abraham,
That our good shepherd would protect each lamb,

All done so that this great Lord we might serve
In holiness, and from Him never swerve.

And you, my precious son, of whom I'm proud,
Shall be God's trumpet, righteous, just and loud.

You shall be called Prophet of the Most High,
Preceding God, of whom you'll prophesy.

You'll make ready His way, teaching salvation,
Preparing them through reconciliation.

His faithful love, which cannot be outdone,
Gives each new day the rising of the Sun

To light our way, in order that each one
Might see light, even those who live in none.

In this dark world, where violence will not cease,
The Son shall guide us to the way of peace."

The child aged and strong his spirit grew,
A desert life before the public's view.

7 An Angel Appears to Joseph
Mt. 1:18-25

When finished caring for Elizabeth,
Then Mary went back home to Nazareth.[15]

Before Mary and Joseph were yet married,
This Joseph learned a child Mary carried.

His heart was broken, as he thought she broke a law,
A sin that could result in death once people saw. [16]

This pious man sought her disgrace to spare,
But thought she must have had a love affair.

He was so filled with hurt, betrayal, blame, and doubt,
That how he should react he could not figure out. [17]

An angel came to Joseph in a dream
And said, "Things are not always as they seem.

You should not fear to take her as your wife,[18]
For in her womb there grows a precious life,

A babe the Holy Spirit did conceive,
To bring a sinful people their reprieve.

Since Yahweh saves,[19] His Son shall bear the name
Of Jesus, for this good news to proclaim."

The reason all of these great things occurred
Was to fulfill the Lord's most holy word

Isaiah spoke,[20] "A maiden undefiled,
Not ever knowing man, will be with child,

For in her womb a little boy will dwell,
And so he shall be called Immanuel,"

Which means "Our God is with us." He awoke
And, word-for-word, did as the angel spoke.

He took his bride-to-be into his house,[21]
Declaring her, to all, to be his spouse,

And, knowing that the Son of God would save,
When Christ was born, the name Jesus he gave.

8 The Birth of Jesus
Lk. 2: 1-7

In those days, Caesar sent out a decree
That said the whole empire enrolled must be,[22]

To count the populace, for so to tax,
To calculate what Rome later ransacks.[23]

"All must go to the place from which they stem!"
The lánúin[24] set out for Bethlehem,

For he was born of David's House and line.
All these events occurred, as by design:

"Oh, Bethlehem, in Judah," Micah said,[25]
"You are not least: from you shall spring the head,

A leader great and without parallel,
Who will shepherd My people Israel."

While there, it came time for Jesus' birth,
The Son of God and, too, a son of earth.

Now, any mother knows the pain she bore,
Much greater than all hurt she knew before,

Yet such a price Mary agreed to pay,
To save mankind, to teach us agape.

So Mary gave birth to this darling boy:
Just as his life, such pain would bring such joy.[26]

In swaddling clothes the newborn babe was wrapped,
And in a manger laid, a place not apt,

But such would He His life on earth begin,
Because there was no place there at the inn.

9 Shepherds Come to Adore the Infant Jesus
Lk. 2:8-20

At this time, in the countryside, nearby,
Shepherds guarded their sheep with watchful eye.

Just then, an angel of the Lord appeared,
And shone God's glory, so the shepherds feared.

"Fear not: we bring good news to fill all with delight,
A joy for the whole people to exult tonight.

Your Christ is born today in David's town,
Though He will have no jewels, nor staff, nor crown,

But swaddling clothes and in a manger laid."
At this, a host of angels serenade,

"Give glory to God in the highest for this birth!
Grant His peace to all those who do His will on earth!"

Now, when the angels back to heaven went,
The shepherds said, "Let's go see this event,

Of which the Lord God has, to us, made known,"
And so they found the king, His humble throne,

And parents proud, just as the angel said.
The news made Mary ponder in her head

What all this meant, for those who heard the tale
Imagined what these signs might all entail.

The shepherds left, to praise and glorify
The God who came to earth to sanctify.

[32]

10 The Circumcision and Presentation in the Temple
Lk. 2:21-38

After a week, just as the law advised
For covenant, the boy was circumcised,

And when the baby was forty days old,
They went to Temple, just as Torah told, [27]

 "Each male who opens up the womb shall be
Consecrated to God eternally," [28]

A gesture to the God who deeply loves.
They offered up a pair of turtledoves· [29]

A righteous man lived in Jerusalem,
Who recognized the fruit from Jesse's stem.

He once was, by the Holy Spirit told,
"In truth, before your body will grow cold,

Your eyes shall see the Lord's anointed one."
So, when they brought to Simeon their Son,

He lifted up the babe and God he blessed.
"Lord, now I know that I, in peace, can rest.

Your servant can, in this young child, see
That You always fulfill Your prophecy.

This light shall be for all a revelation
To bring to Jew and Gentile salvation."

His knowledge left the two of them amazed,
And Simeon, in Mary's eyes, then gazed,

 "For many, He will be the fall or rise,
A sign from God that people will despise,

For to lay bare the hearts who hate the Lord,
While your own heart shall be pierced by a sword."

After his prophesying, there was more.
A prophetess there was, aged eighty-four,

Named Anna, who at Temple always stayed,
Where night and day, she fasted and she prayed.

She came to them and gave sincere thanks to the Lord,
And spoke of Him to all with faith in the Christ stored.

[33]

11 The Visit of the Magi
Lk. 2:21-38

Soon after this came magi from the east,
(A magus is an ancient Persian priest.)

Who said to Herod, "We have seen the sign above,
And came to worship your new king and show our love.

As we will often watch the sky, we saw His star,
So mounted we our camels and have traveled far

To see the young king. Know you where he lies?"
King Herod thought to use the priests as spies.

This threat to Herod's power made him fear,
And those around him, who held power dear.

Their cunning king then held a massive feast,
Where he could ask each learned scribe and priest,

Where would be born, exactly, God's anointed?
They spoke of Micah,[30] so Herod appointed

The magi to report specific news
So he might praise the new king of the Jews.

Thus Herod sent them out to Bethlehem,
And, guided by the star in front of them,

Until, over one place, it came to rest,
Informing them they finished their long quest.

They gave to Him myrrh, frankincense, and gold,
Some pricey earthly gifts, if truth be told.

They, after paying homage to the boy,
Returned home, never having known such joy.

In dreams, angels appeared to truth unveil,
"He will not praise, but sooner would impale

The newborn king. That's why he wants your news.
Your God implores a different road you choose."

And so they went home by another way.

12 Joseph and Mary Flee into Egypt
Lk. 2:21-38

The angel came in Joseph's dream to say,

"Wake up and leave, with Mary and the boy,
For, His young life King Herod would destroy.

Take them to Egypt. Wait for further word."
So Joseph did exactly as he heard.

In order to preserve his child's life,
He left that night, with Jesus and his wife,

Where they would live till King Herod was dead,
Fulfilling what God, through Hosea, said:

"From the land of Egypt I called My son." [31]
With all his cunning, Herod was outdone.

Who thought he had respect from those he ruled
Realized that by the wise men he was fooled.

So mad that they had left without a trail,
He ordered execution for each male

Below age two, as he could calculate,
As from the magi he received the date.

For years, the folk of Bethlehem would be
So overwhelmed with grief and misery,

Like words that were through Jeremiah spoken,
"Our Rachel weeps, her life and spirit broken,

A voice is heard in Ramah, one that's spent
In bitter weeping, sorrow and lament.

No comfort will she let herself receive:
With children dead, all she can do is grieve." [32]

13 The Return to Israel
Mt. 2:19-21

An angel came to Joseph in a dream
Once more. "I've good news of Herod's regime,"

He said, "For Herod and all those who tried
To murder your adopted Son have died.

So take your family to Israel:
The land of milk and honey's safe to dwell."

They went, but soon found out that Archelaus
Inherited his father, Herod's house.

He feared what could befall his family,
Until a dream said, "Go to Galilee."

Thus they could live without the fear of death,
Once settled in a town called Nazareth.

This prophets had, in days long gone, foreseen,
When they wrote, "He'll be called a Nazarene."[33]

14 Jesus' Childhood in Nazareth
Mt. 2:22-23, Lk. 2:39-40

In youth, He gave such joy to all He'd see,
Emitting agape and joie de vie. [34]

In good times, Jesus played and sang and danced, [35]
And when He suffered, wisdom was enhanced. [36]

For from His task on earth, He ne'er would waver,
Forever living life in Yahweh's favor. [37]

15 The Boy Jesus in the Temple
Lk. 2:41-52

They went to David's city[38] each Passover.
When Christ was twelve and when the feast was over,

His parents left, with Jesus left behind:
To check the company had slipped their mind.

They searched among their friends and kin, when one day passed.
When they had found Him not, they headed back, and fast.

In three days, He was in the Temple found.
His parents were exhausted and spellbound,

For He was there with elder, teacher, scribe,
And no one knew where to His depth ascribe.

He asked some questions and gave answers, too,
Which shocked them that so much a young boy knew.

She said, "Why have You treated us this way?!
We've searched for You in fear day after day!"

He said, "How did you search? Did you your paths retrace?
Did you not know I must be in My Father's place?

I must do all My Father does command."
But this His parents did not understand.

They went back home, where Jesus was submissive.
Of these things Mary never was dismissive,

But pondered them, while Christ grew ever wise,
And was revered in men's, and in God's, eyes.

Chapter II
A Voice Cries Out In The Wilderness

16 John the Baptist
Mt. 3: 1-6, Mk. 1: 2-6, Lk. 3:1-6, Jn. 1:19-23

Now, as Isaiah, the prophet, foretold,
"I'm sending out My messenger, behold!

Who shall precede Me and prepare for Me the way,
A voice cries in the wilderness and dares to say,

'Prepare the way of God, make straight His paths!'"[39]
This spoke of John, known for his healing baths.[40]

Then, John preached from Judean desert land,
"Repent! The kingdom of the Lord's at hand!"

In truth, the word of God to John was sent,
Who taught they'd be forgiven who repent.

John wore a garment made of camel's hair
And leather girdle, and his plate was bare,

For he survived on just locusts and honey,
A simple life sans luxuries and money.

They came from far off to the Jordan River
So sinners he could from their sins deliver.

Once all of their transgressions were confessed,
He dunked them and they pledged to do their best.

They died to self as they would hold their breath,
Determined to be sinless unto death.[41]

17 John Preaches Repentance
Mt. 3:7-10, Lk. 3:7-8

When John saw Pharisees and Sadducees,
He told them how they could their Lord God please,

"You brood of vipers! Who gave you instruction
That you must flee the upcoming destruction?

Who cares if faith and deep remorse you've said?
For faith without good works is truly dead. [42]

Do not rely on claims, 'Our father's Abraham!'
As if your God could not your soul forever damn.

It matters not what type of seed is grown,
For God can raise up chosen ones from stone.

Be worried, rather, whether good fruits you provide,
By which a tree's place in the field is justified.

The ax is to the root, the situation dire,
That trees which bear not fruit will go into the fire."

18 John's Advice
Lk. 3:10-14

The multitude asked, "What, then, shall we do?"
John said, "I tell you, anyone with two

Must give away the spare to him who is without.
He with two coats must be in charity devout,

Giving one coat so he without's not cold.
And if you've so much bread that some grows mold,

Give all you don't need to those without any.
Donate excess wealth, every single penny."

And, to the tax collectors, "Don't collect
Unfair amounts you know are not correct.

Collect no more than what's appointed you."
And soldiers asked him, "What are we to do?"

 "Rob none by violence or false accusation,
But be content with what's your compensation."

19 John's Messianic Preaching
Mt. 3:11-12, Mk. 1:7-8, Lk. 3:15-18, Jn. 1: 24-28

Now many asked John, "Are you the Messiah?
Are you the foretold prophet? Or Elijah?"

 "With water, for repentance, I baptize,
But I am not the Christ. One shall arise

Baptizing with the Spirit and with fire,
Who is so great and whom I so admire

That I dare not His sandal strap untie,
In truth, I say, so unworthy am I.

He soon will gather to Himself all wheat,
While chaff will burn in unquenchable heat."

20 The Baptism of Jesus[43]
Mt. 3:13-17, Mk. 1: 9-11, Lk. 3: 21-22, Jn. 1: 29-34

Then Jesus came to John from Galilee,
But John sought not to baptize with this plea,

"No, You should baptize me, rather than I
Give you baptism, yet You've come here. Why?"

"Let it be so; it is My Father's will,
So that all righteousness we may fulfill."

John then consented and Christ was baptized
And, coming from the water, He surprised

The crowds, who saw the heavens open up above
And the Holy Spirit descending like a dove.

And, lo, a voice came telling everyone,
"This man you see is My beloved Son

And with Him I am pleased and well impressed."
To this vision John always would attest.

In truth, the Baptist preached wheree'er he went
And always told about this grand event.

[45]

21 Jesus is Tempted in the Desert
Mt. 4:1-11, Mk. 1:12-13, Lk. 4: 1-13

Through wilderness was Jesus by the Spirit led,
Where He went forty days without a bite of bread,

And, suffering like someone near starvation,
Christ stayed to face the devil's worst temptation.

"If You're the Messiah, the Chosen One,
If You are, as I've heard, God's own dear Son,

Relieve your hunger, making bread from stone.
Then I would know You truly are God's own.

No Son of God should starve, but feast instead."
Christ asked, "What would you know of being fed?

For Scripture said, 'It is not bread alone
By which mankind is nourished, children grown,

But words that prophets speak on God's account.'" [44]
Then Satan took Him to the Temple Mount,

"Jump off the Temple's peak for men to see
The Son of God fulfill the prophecy:

'On rocks, with shattered bones, you shall not land,
But shall an angel bear you in his hand.'"[45]

[46]

"Yet Scripture said, 'You shall not put God to the test.'" [46]
So Satan brought Him to a place above the rest,

And, in an instant, showed every empire.
"Today I offer all You could desire.

For unto me this great world has been given.
Its ways have I made, its course have I driven.[47]

Yes, over this I'll give You full authority,
As it is mine, if You will fall and worship me."

"I cast you out, for scorn's all you deserve!
'The Lord alone shall you worship and serve.'" [48]

So Satan left, until a time more opportune,
And angels came to care for Christ all afternoon.

Chapter III
Jesus Begins His
Public Ministry

22 The Call of the First Disciples[48]
Mt. 4:18-22, Mk. 1:16-20, Lk. 5:1-11

Folks pressed to hear His words, which could the spirit shake,
While Jesus stood right by the Gennesaret Lake.

Just then, He saw two boats unoccupied,
Whose owners washed their nets right alongside.

Christ entered Simon's boat and asked him to
Push out the boat so He the crowd could view.

He preached to them and, when Christ ceased to teach,
He told Simon, "See how far your nets reach.

Let down your nets and you will find a catch."
"Master, if last night's total we could match,

We still would be without a single fish,
But I'll let down my nets, if thus You wish."

On letting down the nets, they were so full
That they called on their friends to help them pull.

Their catch was such the boats were nearly sinking,
And Simon fell down, all his sins rethinking,

"Depart from me, O Lord, for I have been,
As my boat's filled with fish, so filled with sin."

"You need not fear, just do not sin again,
For henceforth your job will be catching men."

The sons of Zebedee, both James and John,
Stood shocked at all they saw there going on.

These three immediately made up their mind
To follow Christ and leave their boats behind.

23 The Wedding at Cana
Jn. 2:1-11

At Cana was a wedding celebration.
Christ and His mother got an invitation,

As well as His disciples. When ran out the wine
She knew they soon would feel the thorn grown by this vine.[49]

She told Him, "They've no wine, while You have power."
He said, "Woman, it is not yet My hour.

What would you have Me do?" And she demanded
The servants do just as Jesus commanded.

Now six stone jars were waiting just nearby,
Which Jews used for themselves to purify,

Which each twenty to thirty gallons carried.
"We must save them distress the day they're married.

Fill them with water. Fill them to the brim!"
They strictly did as they were told by Him.

"Now give the steward of the feast a test."
On tasting it, he said. "This is the best!"

 (Now when the steward drank, he did not know
The change He made the water undergo.)

And to the groom, "Most wait till soberness is past,
And serve bad wine, but you have saved the best for last."

24 Jesus Speaks with Nicodemus
Jn. 3:1-21

Now Nicodemus came, a Pharisee,
Under night's cover,[50] for the Christ to see.

"We know You are a teacher from on high,
For what else could Your power signify?"

And Jesus told him, "What you say is true,
But I tell you one must be born anew[51]

If ever one wants to God's kingdom look upon."
"But how can one be born once from the womb you've gone?

Can one again pass through their mother's womb?
At my age I am closer to my tomb!"[52]

"Lest you are born of Spirit and of water,
You'll not be welcomed as God's son or daughter.

For what is born of flesh is flesh and nothing more;
While those born of the Spirit like a Spirit soar.

[52]

Don't marvel that I said, 'You must be born anew.'
The wind blows though you do not know from whence it blew.

Likewise, those born of spirit freely go.
Their source and goal the worldly do not know."

 "But, Rabbi, how is this all possible?"
"Should not a teacher be with knowledge full?

We speak naught but that of which we have knowledge
And what we've seen we witness and acknowledge

You Pharisees reject our evidence.
If I cannot of earthly things convince,

How will you ever things of heaven learn?
None have gone there, save He who will return.

As Moses in the desert raised the snake,
The Son of Man will be raised for man's sake,

So that the life of those with faith will ne'er be done.
God loves the world so much He gave His only Son

So those with faith in Him would never die,
But always live up with the God Most High.

He came not for to judge, but bring salvation.
Those faithful will not suffer condemnation,

While damned already's he who won't believe,
Who thinks this prophet speaks for to deceive,

Who lacks faith in the name of Yahweh's Son.
Thus shall people be judged for what they've done:

The light was sent, a sun, not just a spark,
But was dismissed since people like it dark.

For evildoers seek to not be seen.
Those hate the light whose actions are obscene.

Those who do deeds that are by God forbidden
Avoid the light to keep transgressions hidden.

Whoever does the truth fears not God's sight,
But loves and even will bask in His light.

25 John Testifies about Christ
Jn. 3:22-36

To the Judean countryside Christ went
Baptizing anyone who would repent.

Now, at this time, near Salim, at Aenon,
Some other people were baptized by John.

Now some of John's disciples and a Jew
Spoke of purification and went to

The Baptist, saying, "Rabbi, now the man
You baptized and bore witness to began

Baptizing. Now all people go to Him."
"The Christ must shine the brighter while I dim.

No one has been given a single thing
That did not from the Lord of heaven spring.

For you can witness, as I've not denied,
I'm not the Christ of whom they prophesied.

I am the one God sent for to prepare the way,
To bring who live in darkness to a bright new day,

To bring them back to God, to be their guide.
Is not the bridegroom he who gets the bride?

And yet, does not the bridegroom's friend rejoice?
Is he not glad at hearing his friend's voice?

His light must grow, while mine must be diminished:
His mission's started while mine's almost finished.

He who comes from above is of the highest worth,
While earthly speech and ways come from the man of earth.

He who comes from above, who is God's Word,[53]
Gives witness to all He has seen and heard.

Although His testimony's oft rejected,
Those who accept it have the rest corrected,

Attesting God is true, since He God sent
Spreads forth His message, just as it was meant.

As God gives Him the Spirit without end.
The Father knows on whom He can depend

And has entrusted all to His beloved Son.
All who believe in Him will have salvation won.

They who refuse belief will not see life,
For God will give them never-ending strife."

Chapter IV
Jesus' Ministry in Galilee

26 Jesus Meets a Samaritan Woman
Jn. 4:1-42

By the time Christ heard Pharisees found out
That He was gaining followers devout,

And more than John the Baptist He baptized,
(Although, in truth, they should have realized

Baptizing was by His disciples done.)
He had his trip to Galilee begun.

Now when someone from Judea goes forth
They pass Samaria, if heading north.

At Sychar, Jesus sat down for to rest
At Jacob's Well, and there His thirst expressed,

Unto a woman (which would folks enrage),
"Might you, dear lady, please My thirst assuage?"

The woman said to Him, "But how can You
Ask this of me, for surely You're a Jew?"

For Jews did not with them associate.[54]
"If you knew how the Lord would compensate,

And who it was who for a drink implored,
You'd ask and living water[55] I'd have poured."

"But You've no bucket and deep is the well.
How would You? Where does living water dwell?

Do You more greatness than our father, Jacob, claim,
Who built it, drank from it, whose sons all did the same?"

"Those who drink here again will need hydration.
My water will last longer than creation

And he who drinks of it will thirst no more,
But, like a spring, give life forevermore."

"An offer such as that I could not spurn.
Please let me drink, that I need not return."

"Bring your husband, that he might drink as well."
"I do not have one." "This is truth you tell.

Although you live with him, you're not his wife,
And you've had five husbands throughout your life."

"I see You are a prophet from the Lord.
I want to know, for there's been much discord,

Since on this mountain we have offered praise,
But you say that the place we ought to raise

Our prayers to God is on the Temple Mount."
"The day will come when both you will discount.

You people worship what you do not know.
We do, for from Jews does salvation flow.

One day you'll neither worship there nor here;
In spirit and in truth you will revere.

Your praise in spirit and in truth God seeks.
He's really not concerned with mountain peaks."

"I know when Christ comes He'll explain all things."
"I am the Christ, God's son, the king of kings."

Then His disciples came back and they saw
Christ talking to a woman. Though in awe,

None of them asked, "Why would You with her speak?"
She nothing now from Jacob's Well could seek,

So she got up, left her jar on the ground,
And told the town how she the Christ had found.

"Come see a man who told me all I've done.
Could He not be the Christ, the Promised One?"

The whole town came out for the Promised One to meet,
Yet His disciples urged him, "Have something to eat."

"I have a food about which you know not."
They wondered who had shared from plate or pot.

"My food consists of doing Yahweh's will.
They say 'Four months till wheat baskets you fill.'

I tell you: Look around. White is the field.
The reaper's bringing in what it will yield,

All for eternal life, so that he may
Rejoice now that he has received his pay,

And with the sower shall he celebrate.
'One sows, another reaps,' as folks relate.

I send you out to reap what you've not sown,
To gain from what you did not plant nor own."

Many Samaritans believed then in God's Son
Because she testified, "He told me all I've done."

They came and begged that He with them remained,
Where by His words, more followers were gained,

For two days preaching, till they testified
To her, "At first, on your words we relied,

But now we've heard and know just what you meant,
That He, to save the world, by God was sent."

27 Jesus Cures a Royal Official's Son
Jn. 4:46b-54

When Christ heard they in chains took John away,
He traveled further north to briefly stay,

Returning to Cana in Galilee
Where He made water wine for all to see.

He came by an official of the court
Who sought a healing as a last resort.

He was distraught, for his son lay in bed
And, sans a miracle, would soon be dead.

"Please come into my house to heal my son.
They say if anyone can, You're the one."

"Sans signs and wonders you will not believe!"
"Please come! My son will die should we not leave."

"Depart and worry not; he shall not die."
The man believed and smiled back, "Good-bye."

While he was walking home, his servants came
All seeking for the good news to proclaim,

"Your son is fine!" "He really is alive!"
"Exactly when did you know he'd survive?"

"'Twas sometime yesterday the fever went away."
"It left him at the seventh hour of the day."

"That is the time the Christ a promise made."
So they believed in Christ and never swayed.

28 Jesus' Preaching at the Synagogue in Nazareth
Lk. 4:16-30

When Christ arrived in Nazareth, where He was raised,
And went into the synagogue, where God was praised,

As was His Sabbath custom, He got up to read,
They have a scroll which He unrolled and thus decreed,

"'God's Spirit is upon me, He's anointed
Me to bring good news to the disappointed,

To heal the broken-hearted and afflicted,
To free captives and those wrongly convicted,

To give sight to the blind and free all those oppressed,
Granting a Sabbath year, of pardoning and rest.'" [56]

He gave them back the scroll and then sat down.
All eyes were on Him, He had such renown.

Then Jesus told them, "Scripture has come true,
As you are listening, in front of you."

Now thus Christ won from those assembled praise,
And gracious from Him was each word and phrase.

[61]

Some said, "Is He not merely Joseph's son?
And His whole family, we know each one:

Is not the woman called Mary His mother?
And Simon, Joe, James, and Jude each His brother?

His sisters are all here with us, likewise.
So how is He so powerful and wise?"

Christ said, "I have no doubt I'll hear you say,
'Physician, heal yourself.' I went away.

You'd be, on hearing what I've done elsewhere,
Demanding I do thus here, to be fair.

No prophet is accepted in his home.
In truth, when Elijah the earth did roam,

There were many widows in Israel,
But, as drought left it dry and hot as hell,

The Lord sent Elijah to Zarephath
In Sidonia as his ordained path.

And, though the Jews had their share of diseases,
Elisha healed none of their sores or sneezes,

And yet Namaan the Syrian was healed."[57]
No hatred or contempt was then concealed.

The crowd sprang up and rushed Him out of town,
Bringing Him to the cliff to throw Him down,

But with them so chaotic, mad, and loud, [58]
Christ walked away, passing straight through the crowd.

29 Jesus Heals a Possessed Man in the Synagogue
Mk. 1:23-28, Lk. 4:33-37

Then going back to Capernaum in Galilee,
He taught on the Sabbath with such authority

That all the synagogue was well impressed.
A man there by a demon was possessed.

He shouted out, as loud as one can shout,
"Have You come here, Jesus, to seek us out?

Have You come to destroy us, every single one?
You are the Holy One of God, His own true Son!"

"Leave from him instantly and you be silent!"
And that damned demon dared not be defiant.

He left the man sans injury or pain,
Which left the crowds unable to explain,

"How have His words such power, such that He commands
Unclean spirits to move without moving His hands?

In whom could such authority reside?"
This news spread all throughout the countryside.

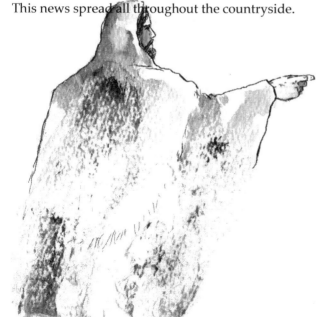

30 The Healing of Peter's Mother-in-Law
Mt. 8:14-15, Mk. 1:29-31, Lk. 4:38-39

And, leaving there, Christ went to Simon's house,
Where sickly was the mother of his spouse.

She lay there fighting back a rising fever,
So they called Christ in hopes He could relieve her.

Jesus stood over her, rebuking the disease,
And she got up to serve, in hopes her guests to please.

31 Multiple Healings That Evening
Mt. 8:16-17, Mk. 1:32-34, Lk. 4:40-41

Now, as sunset drew near, the sick were brought
And each received the healing that they sought.

Some demons came out crying His identity,
But Jesus silenced them and forced them all to flee,

Not wanting to the truth of Him promote.
This all fulfilled what Isaiah once wrote,

"This servant, he took our infirmities
And bore upon himself all our disease."[59]

32 Jesus Leaves Capernaum for Galilee
Mt. 4:23, Mk. 1:35-39, Lk. 4:42-44

Just as the sun began to show its face,
Jesus departed for a lonely place.

There He was followed by an eager crowd,
Who had requests, both numerous and loud.

 "Now I must preach God's kingdom elsewhere, too,
For that is why the Lord sent Me to you."

So Christ walked throughout Galilean land,
Dispelling demons, such was His command,

And going to the synagogues where He would teach,
And everywhere He'd heal the sick and good news preach.

33 The Cleansing of a Leper
Mt. 8:1-4, Mk. 1:40-45, Lk. 5:12-26

In one place, a leper approached the Lord.
He first fell to his knees and then implored,

 "Lord, if You will it, You can make me clean."
Christ pitied this man's pain and quarantine,

And stretched His hand out, touched the man and said,
"I will it." Thus, the leprosy was dead.

But Christ demanded this man who was healed
Keep news about the miracle concealed.

 "But show yourself unto the priest and make
An offering, as proof for people's sake,

As Moses said." Yet news spread all the more
So crowds would follow, such none could ignore.

Christ could not freely travel where they knew
So He into the wilderness withdrew.

34 The Healing of a Paralytic
Mt. 9:1-8, Mk. 2:1-12, Lk. 5:17-26

Returning to Capernaum, His hometown,
A crowd had gathered, He had such renown.

Five men sought Jesus, yet with crowds so vast
They saw Him not, for crowds could not be passed.

They hoped He'd heal their friend, who, paralyzed,
Might have gone home had not one realized

The roof above where Jesus sat could be passed through.
So they lifted him up, removing the roof, too.

On seeing him lowered, their faith made Christ impressed.
He said, "Your sins are pardoned," though none were confessed.

Now when some scribes and Pharisees heard this,
They said, "Only the Lord can guilt dismiss!

A man blasphemes if he makes such a claim!"
Perceiving this, Christ asked them, "Why defame?

What's simpler to say? 'Your sins are forgiven,'
Or 'The power to walk to you is given.'?

To show I have the power to forgive…
Get up! No longer as a cripple live!"

[68]

The man then, without hesitation, rose
And showed the crowd his working knees and toes.

The Lord was by the crowd both feared and glorified,
Who gave authority to someone at their side.

35 The Call of Matthew
Mt. 9:9-13, Mk. 2:13-17, Lk. 5:27-32

He then went out again by the seashore
And taught the crowds who gathered as before.

Christ called out, "Come and follow me!" to Matthew[60]
And he, just like an animated statue,[61]

Got up and left his tax-collecting post,
And they all ate, with Matthew as their host,

With many a sinner and tax collector.
The Pharisees saw Christ as God's defector[62]

And asked, "Why does this man with sinners eat?"
"What doctor would a healthy person treat?

I came to heal the sick, to seek out all those lost.
Learn this: 'I seek mercy and not a holocaust.'[63]

I came to earth not to the righteous call,
But to bring back the sinful, one and all."

36 The Question about Fasting
Mt. 9:14-17, Mk. 2:18-22, Lk. 5:33-39

The followers of John came by to ask
Him about fasting, calling Him to task,

 "Why do we fast, as do the Pharisees,
While your disciples eat just as they please?"

So Jesus questioned them, "What wedding guests would fast
While bride and groom are there? Would they not have a blast?

The days will come when He is here no more.
Then they will fast as any had before.

Who takes a piece of unshrunk cloth to sew
On an old garment? For who does not know

The patch would rip and leave a greater tear?
Likewise, with wine, you all would be aware

That new wine cannot go in old wineskin.[64]
For not long after it would be poured in

The skins would burst and all the wine be spilled.
For both, new wineskins are with new wine filled."

[71]

37 Picking Grain on the Sabbath
Mt. 12:1-8, Mk. 2:23-28, Lk. 6:1-5

One day, Christ and His followers walked past
A field of grain, and having hunger vast,

They started plucking heads of grain to eat.
But Pharisees asked, "Why would You pick wheat

In violation of the Sabbath law?"
"Do you not know what it was written for?

For what did David and his company
Do when they hungered and yet were not free

To eat the bread of the Presence? They ate
Regardless what law it would violate.

Though only priests may eat, the law does mention,
That people starve is not the Lord's intention.

And, on the Sabbath, though the priests profane
The Temple, there is no guilt they obtain.

Now something greater than the Temple's here.
'God wants not sacrifice, but love sincere.' [65]

If you praised thus, instead of just on altars built,
You would not judge someone who does not incur guilt.

Man was not made for Sabbath, but Sabbath for man.
The Son of Man's been Lord of it since it began."

[72]

38 The Man with the Withered Hand
Mt. 12: 9-14, Mk. 3:1-6, Lk. 6:6-11

From there, Christ went into a synagogue,
Where scribes and teachers launched a dialogue,

On seeing someone with a withered hand,
And hoping they the Christ could reprimand.

 "Is it lawful to on the Sabbath heal?"
But from Him they could not their hearts conceal.

 "Which one of you, as owner of a sheep
Which fell into a pit both wide and deep,

Would not do all you could to lift it out?
Each one of you would save it, I've no doubt.

Does not man have more value than a sheep?
So how does one the Sabbath holy keep?

By saving life or letting it expire?"
At this Christ's eyes were filled with such a fire,

While grieved His heart that theirs could be of stone.
Not caring whether praise or rocks were thrown,

He said unto the man, "Stretch out your hand."
The man was healed, since all Christ could command.

The Pharisees went out, with fury filled
And plotted how they might have Jesus killed.

39 Jesus Heals Multitudes by the Sea
Mt. 12:15-21, Mk. 3:7-12, Lk. 6:17-19

Jesus withdrew with His disciples to the sea,
Where he was followed by a crowed from Galilee,

As well as Jerusalem and Judea,
From Tyre, Sidon, and even Idumea.

They sought to see Him, based on all He'd done.
He had His followers, should He need run,

Prepare a boat, the crowd was just so vast.
They all sought to touch Jesus as He passed

So power from Him might their illness heal.
When unclean spirits saw Him, they would kneel

Then fall down, crying out, "You are God's son!"
But Christ ordered they not tell anyone.

This all fulfilled Isaiah's words, "Behold,
My chosen servant greater is than gold.

I love him, for he's faithful and devout.
So I, on him, my Spirit will pour out.

And he'll proclaim justice to all the nations,
But not by loudly screaming declarations.

One solitary bruised reed he'll not break,
Nor shall a quenched smoldering wick he make

Till he wins justice for folks everywhere,
And in his name will Gentiles make their prayer."[66]

40 The Choosing of the Twelve
Mt. 10: 1-16, Mk. 3:13-19a, 6:6b-13, Lk. 6:12-16, 9:1-6

One day, Christ climbed a mountain for to pray
And there, until the next morn, He did stay.

He then called His twelve disciples together
To strengthen them for all that they would weather.

So over demons they received authority
And power for to heal any infirmity.

The twelve apostles' names were James and John,
Peter, the rock the Church was built upon,

His brother, Andrew, and Bartholemew,
Philip, Thomas, the taxman Matthew, too,

And James, who was the son of Alphaeus,
And Judas, also known as Thaddaeus,

And Simon the Zealot, who hated the empire,
And Judas Iscariot, who swapped life for fire.

So Jesus sent the twelve out two by two,
Giving specific orders what to do,

"Avoid Gentiles. Samaritans as well.
Recover the lost sheep of Israel.

Go out and preach, 'The kingdom of heaven's at hand!'
And heal the sick and those possessed throughout the land.

You even shall raise people from the dead.
As I did not charge you for all I've said,

In like ways shall you give it out for free.
When traveling, don't pack like royalty.

Don't carry bags for silver or for gold,
Nor shall you spare tunics or sandals hold,

Nor staff; for laborers, in truth, deserve their food.
When in a town, seek one with a just attitude

And stay with him until you leave that place.
On entering, wish for that house God's grace.

Bestow your peace on them, if they deserve it,
And if they are unworthy, you'll conserve it.

Where'er you go, where they will not receive you,
Shake their dust from your feet so when you leave, you

Show God how they lack hospitality.
Then they'll, for their great immorality,

Far worse than Sodom and Gomorrah burn,
Who made peace from my peacemakers return.

I send you out as sheep with wolves surrounding
So be like doves, in innocence abounding,

And also clever, cunning as a snake."
They left to heal the sick and converts make.

Chapter V
The Sermon on the Mount

41 Occasion of the Sermon
Mt. 4:24-5:2

All over Syria was spread His fame,
For He could cure the sick and demons tame.

They came and He did heal them, and spirits expel,
A crowd that came from all corners of Israel.

He climbed a mountain so that they could see and hear
And spoke in such a way that opened every ear.

42 The Beatitudes[67]
Mt. 5:3-12

"How blest be beggars (in the spiritual sense):
God's kingdom shall be theirs, a kingdom quite immense.

How blest be gentle folk who truly know their worth:
For from their Father they shall inherit the earth.

How blessed, too, one day, shall be those folks who mourn:
They'll gain relief, like mothers when the child's born.[68]

Blest be those who for righteousness hunger and thirst:
They'll get their fill and more, until they almost burst.

Blest be those merciful, who gave reprieve:
The mercy they gave out they will receive.

How blessed be the people pure in heart:
They'll see their God and from Him never part.

Blest be those who God's peace to this world bring:
They shall be recognized as God's offspring.

Blest be those persecuted doing what is right:
God's kingdom shall be theirs, in which they shall delight.

Blest be those who men maltreat and revile,
Spread false rumors about and take to trial,

Endured on My account. I say rejoice,
For prophets paid for using thus their voice."

43 The Salt of the Earth
Mt. 5:13, Mk. 9:49-50, Lk. 14: 34-35

"You are like salt, which carries such a cost.
But what's its worth if all the flavor's lost?[69]

As followers of mine, each grain must be
Forever giving flavor fervently."

44 The Light of the World
Mt. 5:14-16, Mk. 4:21, Lk. 8:16

"For all the world, its light you are to be,
Which is not lit where nobody could see.

A city on a hilltop must be in plain sight.
For who would light a lamp only to waste the light,

By keeping it hidden beneath a table?
Your light must shine, as much as you are able,

That folks will praise the Lord, seeing your deeds.
Your light would then grow flowers bearing seeds[70]."

[81]

45 On the Law and the Prophets
Mt. 5:17-20

"Till all the earth and heavens are destroyed,
None of the Law or Prophets will be void.

I came not to destroy but to fulfill.
Therefore, I warn that anyone who will

Teach others to the Scriptures disregard,
In God's kingdom, will be as low as lard, [71]

While those who virtue do and virtue teach
Will higher be than man could ever reach.

You must outdo the scribe and Pharisee
In virtue for to ever heaven see."

46 On Murder and Wrath
Mt. 5:21-26, Lk. 12: 57-59

"You've heard it said and I will preach it still,
The fifth commandment reads, 'You shall not kill.'

But if your heart be furious and vile,
Hate for your kin will have you sent to trial.

And if your heart be malicious and cruel,
And you should call your brother, 'Worthless fool!'

That pride and malice may send you to hell
For torture doled out by angels that fell.

For sins of cruelty, in whole or in part
Give Satan greater strongholds on your heart.

Make friends of foes and end mutual vice
Before you offer God a sacrifice.

One can't afford to lose in court, I'd think
For judges' fines a sturdy ship could sink.

Make amends out of court and reunite,
For both sides love to end a hurtful fight.

Avoid fights, though temptations may be many,
Or rot in jail sans relief till each penny

In full be paid unto your enemy.
No gain is made from active enmity."

47 On Adultery and Divorce[72]
Mt. 5:27-32

"You've heard, too, 'Don't commit adultery,'
But I say if a lovely girl you see, [73]

And want to sin, so overcome with lust,
Then your own lovely wife misplaced her trust.

To look with lust and on her body dwell
Makes one a sinner[74] on their way to hell.

If your downfall is caused by your right eye,
Then cut it out. Better to live and die

Without one part than your whole person be
Cast in Gehenna[75] for eternity.

Likewise, just cut it off if it's your hand,
Rather than have the whole in hell to land.

You've heard that to divorce a writ you give,
But I say with one woman always live,

Unless unlawful[76] it's already been.
Don't force your wife into a life of sin."

48 On Oaths
Mt. 5:33-37

"You've also heard it said, 'You shall not falsely swear,'
But I say do not swear upon one single hair.

Don't swear by heaven, for that is God's throne,
Nor by the Temple, not one single stone, [77]

Nor by God's holy city, nor his earth.
Your reputation gives your words their worth.

Let 'Yes' mean 'Yes' and let your 'No' mean 'No'.
What's more than this does from the devil flow."

49 On Retaliation
Mt. 5:38-42, Lk. 6:29-30

"You've heard said, 'Tooth for tooth and eye for eye.'
But I say when you're struck, do not rely

On imitation. If one strikes your cheek,
Present the other, so if harm they seek,

They must then your equality assert. [78]
Belike the violent would refrain from hurt.

Likewise, if anyone would steal your coat,
Rather than praying that the Lord will smote,

Give to this man your undergarment, too.
He'd rather run than see that much of you. [79]

And should a soldier make you walk a mile,
Walk with him two, and do so with a smile.

And give to any beggar on the street,
And lend to anyone who does entreat."

50 "Love Your Enemies"
Mt. 5:43-48, Lk. 6:27-28, 32-36, Romans 12:17-21

"You've heard, 'Give love to those who love have earned,
But hatefulness must be with hate returned.'

Nay, bless and pray for people who'll curse and despise,
For, as you lack your Father's wisdom, and His eyes, [80]

Leave vengeance for the Lord, for He will serve
Just punishment upon those who deserve.

It's not your place to other men attack,
But, with your love, win fellow sinners back.

If enemies are starving, give them food!
They'd be so shocked and filled with gratitude,

That they would end the feud, or if one hates, instead,
It would be like pouring hot coals upon his head.

The sun shines on the evil and the just,
So let your kindness shine on all you must.

On good and evil God lets fall the rain.
Don't fall yourself by giving others pain.

What virtue's there, should you love only friends,
For all do this, sometimes towards selfish ends.

If kindness only is reciprocation,
What good is this? Why should that bring salvation?

Don't sinners do the same? And pagans, too?
If you lend to receive, what good have you?

And what if only brethren you salute?
Should God reward a love that's so minute?

Love him who hates and give to him who's broke.
God's kind to selfish and ungrateful folk.

So boundless be your mercy and your love
And you'll be children of your God above."

51 On Almsgiving[81]
Mt. 6:1-4

"Beware, when giving alms, that you not stand
In public view, displaying your right hand,

And sounding trumpets, like the hypocrite
Will do for praise. God knows them counterfeit.

For, even if the gift they can't afford,
These self-righteous have gotten their reward.

When you give alms, your left hand should not know
What does the right. If man's praise you forego,

Only your Father knows what you have done
And, then, reward unending you'll have won."

52 On Prayer[82]
Mt. 6:5-6

"Likewise, don't be like hypocrites in prayer,
Who do so publicly with much fanfare.

They only do so to be seen by men.
When they die, they'll not get reward again.

To pray, go to your room and lock the door.
Then He who sees will blessings on you pour."

53 The Lord's Prayer
Mt. 6:7-15, Lk. 11:2-4

"Don't pray, like pagans, heaping empty phrases.
How would you think Almighty God this phases?

Don't think God cares how many words you say.
He knows your heart, so this is how to pray:

'Our Father dear, who dwells in heaven up above
Your name is sacred and receives our praise and love.

May Your will be done and Your kingdom come,
That here on earth might like heaven become.

When we're in need, O Lord, please keep us fed
And please forgive us all we've done and said,

No more than we our enemies forgive.
All we desire is with our God to live,

Not in the fire down in the lower regions.
Save us from sin and Satan's mighty Legions.'

If you forgive, forgiveness will be yours.
If not, I hope that you are free from flaws."

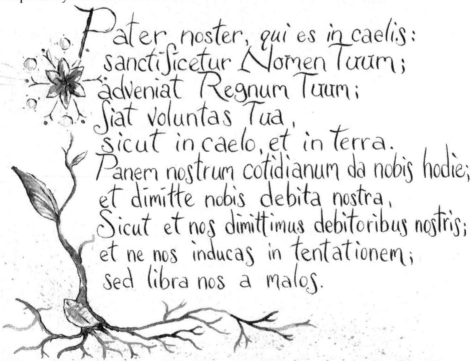

Pater noster, qui es in caelis:
sanctificetur Nomen Tuum;
adveniat Regnum Tuum;
fiat voluntas Tua,
sicut in caelo, et in terra.
Panem nostrum cotidianum da nobis hodie;
et dimitte nobis debita nostra,
Sicut et nos dimittimus debitoribus nostris;
et ne nos inducas in tentationem;
sed libra nos a malos.

54 On Fasting
Mt. 6:16-18

"Don't be like hypocrites, who, when they fast,
Appear in public like their life was past.

For them, reward already was received,
Who make all know their pain need be relieved.

When you fast, wash your face, anoint your head,
So your reward will be from God instead."

55 On Treasures
Mt. 6:19-21, Lk. 12:33-34

"Don't store up wealth in this world to enjoy,
Where moths and worms can eat and rust destroy,

Where purses can grow old and thieves can steal,
But, rather, lay up treasures that are real.

With this wealth, then, when all your life is finished,
You will have treasures which can't be diminished.

You'll rot with money if you cannot part, [83]
For where your treasure is there is your heart."

56 The Sound Eye
Mt. 6:22-23, Lk. 11:34-36

"Amen, I say, the body's lamp's the eye,
Which, when it's sound, it will transmogrify

Your body, making it so full of light.
If not, you've only darkness in your sight.

Then, if your light is dark, how dark will be your days!
But if you're bright, blest be those basking in your rays."

57 On Serving Two Masters
Mt. 6:24, Lk. 16:13

"One cannot be a slave of masters two.
One you'd obey and for one nothing do.

While loving one, the other you'd detest.
You can't serve God and serve a treasure chest."

58 On Anxiety
Mt. 6:25-34, Lk. 12:22-32

"I tell you, don't be anxious for your life,
Nor what you'll eat, nor wear, nor buy your wife. [84]

How much more is your life than what you eat,
Your body more than clothes? How incomplete

Is marriage measured by purchasing power?
Look at the birds and watch the wildflower.

The birds don't sow or reap or gather grain.
Then how much would God go to greater pain

To feed his children, with such higher worth?
Can you add one day to your time on earth?

And what of clothes? Are not the lilies dressed
Better than Solomon, when in his best? [85]

If God so clothes what in the field is grown
And is tomorrow in the furnace thrown,

Will He not clothe you more, O faithless men?
So do not ask, 'What shall we eat, and when?'

'What shall we drink?' 'And what, pray, shall we wear?'
As pagans do; your hearts should be elsewhere.

Your Father up in heaven knows your need.
Seek first the kingdom and your king will feed.

Don't fear tomorning, [86] being filled with doubt.
Today's trouble's enough to fear about.

And know, dear flock, it is your Father's pleasure
To give you His kingdom and share its treasure.[87]"

59 On Judging
Mt. 7:1-5, Mk. 4:24-25, Lk. 6:37-42

"I warn you not to judge, lest judged you be:
Condemn and be condemned eternally.

Only if you forgive you'll be forgiven,
And if you give, it will to you be given.

In truth, whatever standard you employ
The Lord will use for you, for pain or joy. [88]

Why see the speck inside your brother's eye,
While you the log inside your own deny?

How can you tell someone their eye to fix?
You hypocrite, first clear your eye of sticks.

For, then, once you your vision clarify,
You'll see clearly to clean your brother's eye."

60 On Profaning the Holy
Mt. 7:6

"Don't feed the holy food to your canine,
Nor should you throw your pearls in front of swine,

Lest they attack or trample underfoot.
Be careful where the holy things are put."

61 God's Answering of Prayer
Mt. 7:7-11, Lk. 11:9-13

"Seek and you'll find, ask and you shall receive.
Knock and an open door the Lord will leave.

What father, if his son, asked him for bread,
Would give a stone? If he sought fish instead,

What king or father would give him a snake?
If evil men would not, would God forsake

His children so? Would he not comprehend
And unto those who ask the Spirit send?"

62 The Golden Rule
Mt. 7:12, Lk. 6:31

"The law and prophets all say you must do
To others as you'd have them do to you."

63 The Two Ways
Mt. 7:13-14, Lk. 13:23-24

"I tell you you must enter through the narrow gate.
The road to hell leads downhill[89] and its doorway great,

And many walk on it, too weak to climb the height.
The road to life is difficult, its traffic light.

When searching for your road, don't seek the one that's paved.
It's far too often strode and morally depraved." [90]

64 "By Their Fruits You Will Know Them"
Mt. 7:15-20, Lk. 6:43-45

"Beware of prophets false, who dress as sheep,
Though inwardly are wolves. Though blood runs deep,

Where lies their heart can easily be known.
To see the heart, look where the seeds are sewn. [91]

For bad trees grow bad fruit; likewise the good.
And rotten fruit just grows from rotten wood.

For good fruit always grows when trees are sound,
While from the bad trees only bad fruit's found.

Such trees are cut and in the fires tossed.
Thus you will know for sure when sheep are lost."

65 Saying "Lord, Lord"
Mt. 7:21-23

"Not everyone who says to me, 'Lord, Lord,'
Will gain from God everlasting reward,

But only he who does My Father's will.
On that day, they'll say, 'Did we not instill

True faith in You, and those possessed reclaim?
Did we not do great works, all in Your name?'

I will declare to them, 'I know you not,
You wicked men, depart from me and rot.'"

66 The House Built On Rock
Mt. 7:24-27, Lk. 6:47-49

"The one who listens and is free of guilt
Is like he who on rocks his house has built.

The rains came down and caused a massive flood,
But neither wind nor rain nor running mud

Could make it fall, because of its foundation.
Now one who hears and makes no alteration

Is like the fool who built his house on sand.
The coming storm his house could not withstand.

The winds and rain tore his house to the ground
With ease, since his foundation was not sound.

When homes collapse, then, how great is the fall!"

67 The Effect of the Sermon
Mt. 7:28-29

Those hearing these were impressed by it all.

In teaching, He authority commanded.
The scribes stood silent, as if reprimanded.

Chapter VI
Jesus Continues His
Ministry in Galilee

68 The Faith of the Centurion
Mt. 8:5-13, Lk. 7:1-10

On entering Capernaum, Jesus met
Some elders of the Jews who hoped to get

A healing for the slave of a Gentile.
For this man heard a rumor most worthwhile

Of healings Jesus did, while his beloved slave
Was on death's door. He hoped Christ would his servant save.

The elders told him, "He's a worthy man
Who loves our nation. Please do what you can,

For this centurion even erected
Our synagogue, and this has so effected

This man. Please come with us to do a healing."
So Christ agreed, compassion always feeling.

When not far from his home, the man came out
And told the people, "Stop! I have no doubt,

For I have many soldiers under my command.
So how authority works out I understand.

If I say 'Go,' they go or 'Do' they do,
And so much more must all things obey You.

I don't deserve to have You come to me.
Just speak and healed will my sick servant be."

On hearing all this, Jesus was in awe.
"So much belief I truly never saw,

Not even anywhere in Israel.
In truth, some Jews will rot always in hell,

While those from south and north, from west and east
With Abraham and Israel shall feast.

Depart. It has been done as you beseeched."
At that instant, His healing power reached.

69 The Raising of the Widow's Son
Lk. 7:11-17

Soon hence, Christ went to Nain, a nearby city
With quite a crowd, and soon was filled with pity,

For, by the city gate, a man who died
Was carried while his mother loudly cried.

She was a widow with a crowd around her
And Jesus, filled with mercy when He found her,

Implored the weeping widow, "You must weep no more."
And walked to the deceased, with new life to restore.

He said to him, "Young man, I say, arise!
Get up from there and dry your mother's eyes."

The dead man got up, leaving them in awe,
Such that the crowd, in sync, each dropped their jaw.

Christ gave him to his mother; they were filled with fear
And glorified the Lord, "A great prophet is here!"

"God visited His people, Israel."
News spread through Judea and north as well.

[108]

70 On Following Jesus
Mt. 8:18-22, Lk. 9:57-62

While Jesus and a crowd walked down the road,
A man from the other direction strode,

And called to Christ, "I'll follow You where'er You go!"
"I warn you where I sleep tonight I do not know.

A fox will have its hole, a bird its nest.
The Son of Man has nowhere for to rest."[92]

He told one, "Follow Me," but that man said,
"I must first bury my father instead."[93]

"Let dead men bury those who are deceased.
You, preach the kingdom north, south, west, and east."

"I'll follow You, immediately after
I tell my household I'll be gone hereafter,"

Another said, but Christ warned, "No one who
Begins to push the plough, yet can't get through,

For they are too distracted, looking back,
Can enter heaven, since focus they lack."

[109]

71 Two Blind Men Regain their Sight
Mt. 9:27-31

Soon after this, as Christ was passing by,
Two blind men followed Him, and they did cry,

"Have mercy, we beseech You, David's Son!"
"Do you believe by Me this can be done?"

"Yes, Lord, we know the great power You wield."
"According to your faith shall you be healed."

They saw, but Christ warned, "Don't tell anyone."
Yet they told everyone under the sun.

72 The Dumb Demoniac
Mt. 9:32-34

As Christ left, He was met by a request
To heal a man who spoke not since possessed.

When it was cast out, this man spoke again,
Which left the crowd astonished, asking, "When

Has such a thing been seen in Israel?"
Yet Pharisees claimed, "His power's from hell."

73 The Harvest is Great
Mt. 9:35-38

Then Jesus traveled throughout town and city
And healed all those who merited His pity,

While everywhere He went the gospel spread.
The crowd was like a body sans a head

Or like some sheep that were a shepherd lacking.
He said, "The harvest you should all be packing,

For it is plentiful with labors few.
Pray God sends workers for it all to do."

74 Open and Fearless Speech
Mt. 10:26-33, Lk. 12:2-9

"There's nothing covered that won't be revealed
And nothing hidden may remain concealed.

What's whispered nightly shout throughout the day.
Proclaim on rooftops everything I say!

Fear not who kills the flesh, but not the soul as well.
Be scared of Him who throws both flesh and soul in hell.

In truth, two sparrows sell for just a penny
And God knows every one. However many

Hair follicles are on your head God knows the count.
And you're worth more than birds, by such a great amount!"

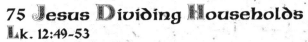

75 Jesus Dividing Households
Lk. 12:49-53

"I've come to earth to set the world afire.
That it were blazing now do I desire!

By other means must I still be baptized
And am constrained until this is realized.

Think you I came to earth to bring it peace?
I brought a sword that unity might cease.

For henceforth shall each household be divided,
With three verse two based on how each one sided:

Father verse son and brother verses brother,
Sister verse sister and daughter verse mother,

With people always feuding with their kin,
From whom the greatest danger they'll be in."

76 Renouncing Self for Jesus and its Rewards
Mt. 10:37-39, Lk. 14:25-33

"Who has more love for father or for mother
Or son or daughter, or for any other,

Than he has for Myself does not deserve
A life with Me. He must his master serve.

Whoever will not die upon a cross,
But saves his life will know far greater loss.

Who saves his life will not see life unending;
Who gives it will to heaven be ascending.

Before you'd build a tower, you would count the cost,
Lest when the funds run out, all you have spent is lost.

Then everyone in town would ridicule,
'You started and could not finish, you fool!'

Or, then, what king, when setting out to war,
Does not ask if his enemy has more?

Then, seeing he's outnumbered, this king might
Gain decent terms, as he can't win the fight.

Before you try to build My church without a stone,
Do not commit lest you renounce all that you own.

He who receives you in receives Me, too,
And welcomes He who sent Me here to you.

He who receives a prophet for his word
Will get reward like he the masses stirred.

Who welcomes holy men because they're just
Will gain a just man's prize; this they can trust.

Who has, for one, a cup of water poured,
Because they follow Me, will gain reward."

When Jesus finished his disciples teaching,
He went from these to nearby cities preaching.

77 John the Baptist's Question and Jesus' Answer
Mt. 11:2-6, Lk. 7:18-23

When John the Baptist heard, from prison, of Christ's deeds,
His messengers asked, "Are you all Israel needs?

Are you the savior whom the Lord foretold
Or is another meant to lead God's fold?"

At that hour, He gave the blind their sight,
Cured illnesses and made demons take flight.

He answered, "Tell him what you've heard and seen:
The blind are made to see and lepers clean,

And those with different illnesses are healed,
While power to cast demons out I wield.

The deaf hear while people rise from the dead,
But, mostly, good news to the poor is said.

Tell John what you make of the evidence.
Blest be who hear and do not take offense."

78 Jesus' Witness concerning John
Mt. 11:7-19, Lk. 7:24-35

When John's disciples left, Christ asked the crowd,
"What did you go to see? A reed that bowed,

Blown by the wind, deep in the wilderness?
A man who dressed for eyes or lived for bliss?

Such people do in palaces reside.
Instead, you went to where a prophet cried.

As it is written, John is a prophet and more:
'I show my face, but send a messenger before

Whose job is to prepare the way for Me.' [94]
There's never been better, I guarantee,

From women born, both living and deceased.
Yet next to those from heaven he'd be least.

Towards John the Law and prophets prophesied
And, as you know, Elijah never died.[95]

Well, John the Baptist, if you will believe,
Is the Elijah for My coming's eve.

[118]

Let anyone by whom this may be heard,
Listen and take heed unto every word,

Reflecting closely till they understand
The word of God like the back of their hand

Who heard him, even in the tax collector's case,
Acknowledged, through John's baptism, God's saving grace.

The Pharisees and lawyers this refused:
By spurning God's plan shall they stand accused.

To whom shall I compare this generation?
Like children sitting, shouting from frustration,

 'We played our pipes and yet you did not dance!
We wailed and yet your tears did not advance!'

For John would not feast or have heavy drink
And some said, 'He's possessed, I surely think.'

Yet since the Son of Man feasts and has wine,
They say, 'He drinks like drunkards, eats like swine.[96]

He eats with those who should be cast aside.'
Yet wisdom's by her children justified."

79 "I Will Give You Rest"
Mt. 11:28-30

"Come unto Me, you weary, heavy-laden.
I'll help you as all men would help a maiden,

For who will take my yoke I will give rest.
I'm gentle, humble, and I aid the stressed.

For, though the day is rough and dark's the night,
My yoke is easy and my burden light."

80 The Woman with the Ointment
Lk. 7:36-50

While Jesus visited, in Bethany,
Simon, a leper and a Pharisee,

A woman who was hoping she would meet Him
Came up to Christ and showed all how to treat Him.

She was a sinner with that reputation
Who mourned how she had fallen to temptation.

She feared God's wrath, or maybe disappointment,
And poured an alabaster flask of ointment

Upon His feet and washed them with her hair.
Yet Simon wondered why He let her there.

He said, "Were He a prophet, as they say,
He'd know her sins and have her sent away."

"Simon! I've something urgent I must say to you."
"Then, teacher, speak." "A creditor had debtors two.

For one debtor, fifty denarii was his debt,
The other ten times this. When payments were not met,

The man forgave them both. I ask which debtor
Would love him more? Which one would thank him better?"

"The one, I'm sure, who'd been forgiven more."
"Of course. Look at this woman on the floor.

I came and got no water for My feet,
While she has given them a bath complete.

She washed them with her tears and dried them with her hair.
You gave no kiss, while she gave all that she could spare.

While you did not with oil anoint my head
This woman anointed My feet instead.

She is forgiven for her love is great.
For those forgiven less far less prostrate."

Christ said, "Forgiven is your every sin."
And, though this made from ear to ear her grin,

Some asked each other, "Who can such a power claim?"
Christ said to her, "Shalom! Your faith has quelled your shame."

81 The Generous Women who Walked with Jesus
Lk. 8:1-3

Christ preached through many towns and cities all around.
The twelve and women who were always with them found

Were his companions and this group included
One healed when seven demons had intruded

Called Mary Magdalene. With her, Suzanna
And Herod's steward Chuza's wife Joanna,

And others, who had from their wealth donated
So that the needs of all their group were sated.

82 Jesus' True Kindred
Mt. 12:46-50, Mk. 3:31-35, Lk. 8:19-21

While Jesus was still to a vast crowd speaking,
His mother and His brothers came there seeking

His audience, and this the crowd relayed,
Expecting Him to leap and yet He stayed.

 "Who is my mother? Who's my family?"
He stretched His hand towards them, "They're here with Me!

You are my kin," He told the crowd and smiled,
"Those who obey My Father like His child."

83 The Parable of the Sower
Mt. 13:1-9, Mk. 4:1-9, Lk. 8:4-8

Christ went out by the sea later that day,
Then in a boat to keep the crowd at bay.

While He sat down, the crowd stood on the beach.
Christ saw their need and so began to teach:

"A sower went out sowing in his field,
With hopes of an abundant crop to yield.

Some seeds fell where the soil met the road,
And so were underneath where people strode

Or laid there and by hungry birds were found.
Some other seeds fell onto rocky ground.

With little dirt, they sprang up right away,
But lacked the depth of dirt plants need to stay.

The scorching sunlight they could not withstand,
For dry a plant can't bear the Sun's demand.

Some fell on thorns, which grew to choke the seed:
So many seeds could never grow to feed.

Some fell on great soil, producing grain
That would give to the sower such a gain,

Of thirty, sixty, or a hundredfold,
A treasure worth more than its weight in gold.

Let anyone by whom this may be heard,
Listen and take heed unto every word,

Reflecting closely till they understand
The word of God like the back of their hand." [97]

84 The Reason for Speaking in Parables
Mt. 13:10-17, Mk. 4:10-12, Lk. 8:9-10

Disciples asked, "Why is it that you speak
In parables to give them what they seek?"

Christ said, "Wisdom to you has been outpoured
To know about the kingdom of the Lord.

For he who has will keep receiving more,
And those without will grow forever poor.

For those who've taken Yahweh's Law to heart,
The parables will more wisdom impart,

While those who took God's Word just to misuse,
Will hear these and it greater will confuse. [98]

They make God's law a pointless, strict law code.
It was designed to bring folks to the road[99]

To walk in life, that of unselfish love,
To lead them to the life with God above.

For those expecting guaranteed inheritance
'Cause they can walk, no words I could say could convince.

It is exactly like Isaiah said,
'The words you hear will be lost in your head,

And what you see you never will perceive.
These people have chosen to be naïve.

They've closed their eyes and ears with hardened hearts,
Lest they should see, for then wisdom imparts

Insight into exactly who they've been
And how they've lived their lives so full of sin.

They'd then repent and turn back to the Lord
To have their spiritual health restored.'

But blessed be your eye and blessed be your ear!
For prophets and righteous men longed to see and hear

What you have. Truly they would be so jealous.
This revelation should make hearers zealous!"

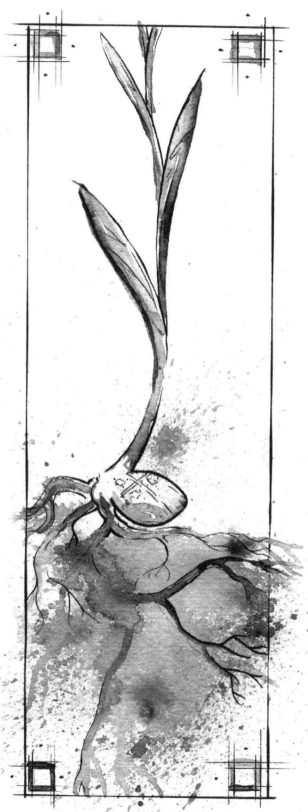

85 Interpretation of the Parable of the Sower
Mt. 13:18-23, Mk. 4:13-20, Lk. 8:11-15

"In case the message you don't understand,
The symbolism I will now expand:

In it, the sower sows God's holy word
And Satan's represented by the bird

Who takes away what's sown into his heart,
Who hears but only understands in part.

And those on rocky ground receive with joy
God's word, but like a boy with a new toy,

They have no roots and when there comes temptation,
Or when the word will bring them tribulation,

They lack the strength for to endure the storm.
And what of seeds who fall among the thorn?

They are the ones who live to please the self.
For, choked by love of pleasure and of pelf, [100]

They never give the world a single fruit.
Whether they ever cared, the point is moot.

Yet he who holds true to the word will yield
As much fruit as would an entire field!"

[128]

86 "He who has Ears to Hear, Let him Hear"
Mk. 4:23

"Let anyone by whom this may be heard,
Listen and take heed unto every word,

Reflecting closely till they understand
The word of God like the back of their hand."

87 The Parable of the Seed Growing Secretly
Mk. 4:26-29

"God's kingdom can be likened to a man,
Who scattered seed to grow, as was his plan.

He woke and slept, while seeds grew o'er the land.
Yet, how they grew he did not understand.[101]

The land gave fruit, all of its own accord.
The plants, from shoot to ear, to heaven soared!

Then when the crop is ready, he will reap
And gather them, as shepherds would their sheep." [102]

88 The Parable of the Good and Bad Seed
Mt. 13:24-30

"The kingdom's like a man who sowed good seed,
Whose enemy then sowed many a weed

Amongst the wheat, all while the farmer slept.
Then those servants by whom the field was kept

Asked him, 'What kind of seed, sir, did you sow?
For, there, among the good plants bad ones grow.

Should we gather those that should not be there?'
'If you did that, how would my good seed fare?

They'll grow together till it's harvest time.
To judge them all the same would be a crime,

Just like the man who sowed the wicked seed,
An enemy consumed by hate and greed.[103]

When harvest comes, bring to my barn my wheat,
While weeds will be consumed by flames and heat.'"

89 The Parable of the Mustard Seed
Mt. 13:31-32, Mk. 4:30-32, Lk. 13:18-19

"With what else can God's kingdom be compared?
'Tis like a mustard seed," Christ then declared.

"The smallest of the seeds when it is sown,
But greatest of all shrubs once it has grown,

So large its branches hold a small bird's nest,
Where she can hatch her young and let them rest."

90 Jesus' Use of Parables
Mt. 13:34-35, Mk. 4:33-34

So much did He use parables to teach the crowds
That He was seen as linked to them as rain to clouds.[104]

In this way He instructed them as they could hear,
But then ensured to His disciples all was clear.

This way fulfilled what prophets long had spoken,
"In speaking parables will my mouth open,

Thus making clear what hidden was from men,
What they have not known since the world began."

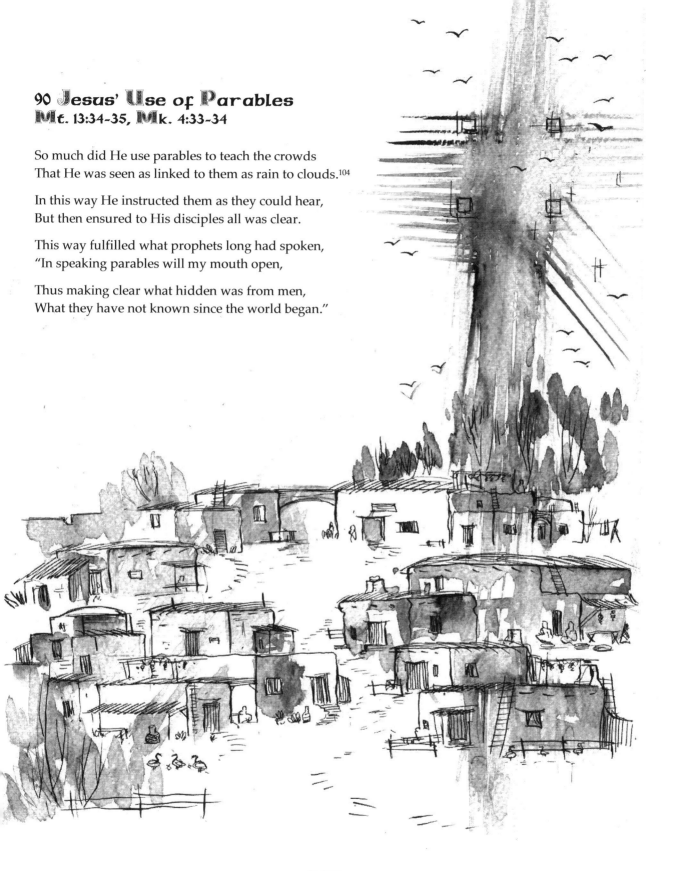

91 Interpretation of the Parable of the Good and Bad Seed
Mt. 13:36-43

"The sower's enemy's the Evil One,
Through whom all malice and deceit is done.

The sower is the Son who is revealed,
And Earth is represented by the field.

The weeds are slaves who serve the Evil One,
While good seed serves the Father and the Son.

When harvest time comes, that is the world's end.
Its reapers are those angels who are friend

To God, who gladly follow His commands,
Against whom no servant of sin withstands.

Just as the weed must be fuel for the fire,
So to who evil do or do inspire.

The angels will into the furnace throw
The wicked, while the just like stars[105] will glow.

Let anyone by whom this may be heard,
Listen and take heed unto every word,

Reflecting closely till they understand
The word of God like the back of their hand."[106]

[134]

92 The Parables of the Hidden Treasure and of the Pearl
Mt. 13:44-46

"The kingdom's like a treasure in a field,
But buried and the place to one revealed.

He covers it and sells all that he owns,
To buy the dirt, for gold and precious stones.

Again, it's like a man who searches for
Great pearls in every marketplace and store.

He found a great one. All he had was sold
To buy a pearl worth his whole weight in gold.

Such efforts will men make to get their treasures."

93 The Parable of the Leaven
Mt. 13:33, Lk. 13:20-21

"For heaven is like leaven in three measures

Of flour (where all women put their yeast).
The leavened bread then grew for such a feast!"

94 The Parable of the Net
Mt. 13:47-50

"The kingdom of heaven is like a net
That was thrown in the sea as the sun set.[107]

The net then gathered fish of every kind
And fishers did as they are all inclined.

Once full, the fishers hauled the net ashore
And threw away whose tastes people abhor.

Once useless ones were gone, the good were placed
In baskets that were delicately laced.

So 'twill be when the world comes to an end:
God's angels separating foe from friend,

95 Treasures New and Old
Mt. 13:51-52

"Do you grasp this: the pearl, the seed, the leaven?"
"We do." "Then every scribe now trained for heaven

Is like a man with treasure new and old,
With each one highly valued when they're sold."

96 Stilling the Storm
Mt. 8:23-27, Mk. 4:35-41, Lk. 8:22-25

One day, at dusk, Christ told all those beside,
"Let us set sail to reach the other side."

And so they left the crowd and left the shore.
In minutes, Jesus was awake no more.

Then o'er the lake there came a massive storm,
Such that they woke the Lord up to inform,

"O, Teacher, we will perish certainly.
Do you not care our boat fills with the sea?"

So He awoke, rebuking wind and rain,
"Be still at once!" and neither dared remain.

"Where is your faith at? Why are you afraid?"
They marveled then, "The wind and sea obeyed!

Who then is this, that He has such command?"
Each stood in awe, and tried to understand.

[139]

97 The Gerasene Demoniacs
Mt. 8:28-34, Mk. 5:1-20, Lk. 8:26-39

Across the lake, where men were Gerasene,
Christ met one with a spirit most unclean,

A man possessed who lived among the graves,
Who they could not bind, as men did with slaves.

When they did, chains and fetters he would break,
So trips that passed by him no one would make.

Among the tombs and on the mountain peak,
All day and all night long would this man shriek,

While taking stones with which himself to beat.
On seeing Christ, he fell down at His feet,

 "What do You want with me, Son of the God Most High?
Please do not torture me, your wrath to satisfy!"

For he was told by Christ he must depart.
"What name for you did Lucifer impart?"

 "The name earned by us in his lowest region,
We bear the name that makes blood flow: we're Legion.[108]

Oh, please, we beg that You not just dismiss,
Sending us to the dark endless abyss."

A herd of swine was feeding on the hillside there.
"Let us enter the swine and this man we will spare."

So Jesus gave them leave and they entered the herd,
Which then flew down the cliff, each like a dying bird,

Into the sea, where all two thousand drowned.
The herdsmen fled and told this all around.

So crowds came to see Jesus, who had stayed
With him He cured, though this made them afraid.

Though he was clothed and now in his right mind,
The people were not towards kindness inclined.

They begged that Christ would leave their neighborhood.
And so the man He healed asked if he could

Leave there with Jesus, though Christ said instead,
"Return to both your friends and your homestead,
And tell them all the Lord for you has done,
To someone feared and loathed by everyone."

Through the Decapolis did he proclaim
How great was Christ that demons He could tame.

98 Jairus' Daughter and the Woman with a Hemorrhage
Mt. 9:18-26, Mk. 5:21-43, Lk. 8:40-56

When Christ came in a boat, across the lake,
He met Jairus, a man filled with heartache,

A ruler of the synagogue, who pled,
"Please help my daughter lest she soon be dead!

My little girl will not long be alive
Lest You lay hands on her for to revive."

So Jesus followed him, as did a crowd.
Yet, then, a woman through the masses plowed.

(She had a hemorrhage for twelve long years,
Which caused huge doctors' bills and many tears,

And just got worse. She heard Christ could demons dispel
And said, "If I just touch His clothing, I'll be well.")

She touched His robe and instantly was healed,
But this could not from Jesus be concealed.

On feeling power leave Him, He called out,
"Who touched Me? Someone did, I have no doubt."

Said Peter, "Master, with this multitude,
How could we know with any certitude,

Since they press down upon you?" "I perceive
One touched My clothes; then did My power leave."

He looked and she knew she could not stay hidden
And feared that she had done something forbidden.

She came forth, falling down, with trembling voice,
And told the truth. Christ said, "Daughter, rejoice!

Your faith has made you well; now, go in peace.
The suffering you've long endured shall cease."

While he was speaking, messengers brought word,
"My lord, your worst nightmare has just occurred.

Your daughter died, so trouble Him no more."
"Have faith and she'll be as she was before."

[142]

When Jairus' household they came upon,
He entered with just Peter, James, and John,

And saw the chaos: mourning, wailing, weeping.
He asked, "Why cry? Colleen[109] is only sleeping."

They all laughed, knowing that the girl was dead.
So, with her parents, He went to her bed.

He took her hand and said, "Colleen, arise."
She rose up, walking, to their great surprise.

He ordered they give her something to eat.
He charged them to tell no one of this feat,

And yet, despite all this that Jesus said,
Throughout the district news of it was spread.

99 The Healing at the Pool
Jn. 5:2-47

A Jewish festival[110] occurred right after this.
Christ went down to Jerusalem so not to miss

The yearly miracle and the fiesta
Which happened by the pool they called Bethesda.[111]

There lay the blind, the lame, the paralyzed.
Christ saw one man and deeply empathyzed,

For he had suffered thirty-eight long years.
Christ knew it caused much shame and many tears

And asked, "Would you like to be well again?"
"Of course I would, and I do what I can.

But I have no one who will throw me in.
When it's disturbed, the race I never win."

"Get up, pick up your mat, and walk around."
The crippled man his miracle then found.

[144]

Now since this happened on the Sabbath day,
The Jews who witnessed this began to say,

"You cannot on the Sabbath move your mat."
"The man who cured me told me to do that."

"Who said, 'Take up your mat and walk with it.'?"
"I do not know the man, I must admit."

He did not know, so crowded was the place.
Then, in the Temple, they met face-to-face.

Christ said, "I'm glad to see that you are well.
Don't sin or you shall know far greater hell."

The man gave testimony to the Jews
And for this Sabbath work did they accuse

The Christ of sin, and they harassed Him, too.
"If work today My Father did not do,

Earth would collapse and life on it would end.
Does not the angel work and then ascend?

When fathers work their sons must work as well."
Since He had made Himself God's parallel,

That made them more intent the Christ to kill.
"The Son acts not of His power or will,

But all He does He's seen the Father's done.
Now so much does the Father love the Son

That He has shown Him all He does and more will show,
Such that your minds could neither understand nor know.

[145]

For, as the Father gives life to the dead,
He judges not, but lets His Son instead,[112]

And lets Him give men life at will, so people may
As to the Father, praise the Son in the same way.

He who refuses honor to the Son
Dishonors Him who sent the Promised One.

Yet they who listen and My words obey
And, in the One who sent Me their faith lay,

Will find judgment a thing they can avoid.
They'll live forever, always overjoyed.

In truth, the time is coming – nay, I say, it's here
When those who've died will hear the Son's voice in their ear,

And all who listen to My voice will always live.
For Yahweh did His own life-giving power give

Unto the Son of Man, to judge the world,
Deciding who into Gehenna's hurled.

Now soon those who did good will leave their graves,
Once they have listened to the Son who saves,

While evildoers face a horrid fate.
I cannot by Myself judgment dictate,

But use the standard Yahweh did instill,
A judgment just, seeking My Father's will.

If only I could testify on My behalf,
Then any claim to boost My name would make men laugh.

One testifies to what I am about
Whose credibility no one could doubt.

Though testimony I received from John,
The words of men I don't rely upon.

I only mention it for your salvation.
John was a lamp and his illumination

Made people once content, to see his light.
But greater testimony in your sight

Was given by My Father through My deeds.
Each miracle a source of power needs.

Besides, the Father bears witness to Me,
Although the Father's form you do not see,

Nor hear His voice, for in you His words cannot find
A home, as pleas to put faith in Me were declined.

You study Scriptures, thinking there will be
Eternal life. They testify to Me,

And, yet, to always live you'll not come here.
It does not mean a thing if men revere,

For human glory truly has no worth.
Besides, I know too well you men of earth

Who have no love for God, the Lord Most High.
Hence My message and My words you deny,

Though in the name of My Father I came.
If someone else should come, in his own name,

You would accept him. How can you believe,
Since you seek glory in how men perceive,

And care not for the glory from on high.
Moses is he upon whom you rely

And, to the Father, Moses will accuse.
If you had faith in him, you'd not refuse

Belief in Me, since it was I he wrote about.
You don't believe his words; of course you're filled with doubt."

100 Opinions Regarding Jesus
Mt. 14:1-2, Mk. 6:14-16, Lk. 9:7-9

At that time, Herod the tetrarch had heard
How sick and blind were cured and crowds were stirred.

His council was divided and some said,
"It's John the Baptist risen from the dead,"

While others claimed, "Elijah has returned."
"Or some other prophet whose wrath we've earned."

"It's John the Baptist, whom I had so dreaded,
Raised from the dead, though I had him beheaded."[113]

101 The Death of John the Baptist
Mt. 14:3-12, Mk. 6:17-29, Lk. 3:19-20

For Herod had the Baptist seized and bound,
Who had made condemnations most well-found,

For Herod and Herodias were wed.
She was his brother's wife and, as John said,

"It is not lawful that you be with her."[114]
Though Herod liked it when they would confer,

John was by Herodias so despised
She sought his death because he criticized.

Since John was as a prophet seen throughout the land,
He killed him not, and though he did not understand

The words he spoke, he gladly would hear John.
Now, while imprisonment was undergone,

King Herod had a massive birthday party
Where wine flowed freely and the meat was hearty.

Herodias' daughter danced in such a way
It so beguiled Herod he heard himself say,

"I'll grant you anything that you wish for,
Half of my kingdom, even, but no more."

Surprised, she sought her mom out. "What's the matter?"
"What shall I ask for?" "John's head on a platter."

Though he deeply regretted such an oath,
He did not want to disappoint them both,

Especially among assembled guests,
Lest they think he won't grant promised requests.

And so John lost his head to grant her wish,
To have it served upon a silver dish.

The girl then to her mom his head presented
And the Judean countryside lamented.

His followers came by, hoping to bury,
And brought his corpse into the cemetery.

[149]

102 The Return of the Apostles
Mk. 6:30-31

The twelve came, telling all they'd done and taught
And also news of John the Baptist brought.

Distraught, Christ sought some sort of consolation,
So flee did He to be in isolation.

 (To be with His apostles, but no crowd,
Which tend to be stressful, needy, and loud.)

103 Five Thousand are Fed
Mt. 14:13-21, Mk. 6:32-44, Lk. 9:10b-17, Jn. 6:1-15

Crowds saw Him sail and followed Him behind,
Outpacing Him; hence, He could not unwind.

Christ pitied them and wanted to bestead
Who were like sheep not by a shepherd led.

He taught the gospel and he cured their ill.
Then He was told by his apostle, Phil,

 "This place is lonely and late is the day.
By now, you must send this vast crowd away."

 "They need not. You give them something to eat."
"But, Lord, for to accomplish such a feat,

Would two hundred denarri cost, at least!
And that's just for a mouthful, not a feast."

 "A lad here has five barley loaves and fish,"
Andrew spoke out, "We'll split them as you wish,

Though, honestly, I do not really know
How far five loaves and two mere fish can go."

Christ said, "Have all of them sit on the grass
And watch as we shall feed them all en masse."

Christ took the loaves and fish and looked up to the sky.
He blessed and broke the bread, which He did multiply

So when, through His apostles, He passed out the bread,
They could, with bread and fish, make sure that all were fed.

Christ said, "Gather what's left so nothing's lost."
Fragments into twelve baskets full were tossed.

 (The crowd He fed numbered five thousand men,
Plus wives and kids who were not counted then.)

Once people could His power and His love behold,
They said, "This is the world's great prophet, long foretold."

Knowing that they would make Him king, He ran
Into the mountains to fulfill God's plan.

104 The Walking on the Water
Mt. 14:22-33, Mk. 6:45-52, Jn. 6:16-21

Now Christ went to the mountaintop alone,
Avoiding living on a man-made throne.

He bade ahead of Him that His apostles leave
And He would catch up after He had time to grieve.

When finished praying, Christ went to the shore
And watched them fight the wind and waves with oar.

Then, at around the fourth watch of the night,
They saw a thing that made them doubt their sight.

For they saw Jesus on the water tread.
"It is a ghost! We're haunted by the dead!"

So Jesus told them, "Take heart, it is I."
Peter replied, "If that's You, I'll comply

Should You tell me to walk with You out there."
"Come here." And walk he did till wind did scare.

For once the wonder of it made him think,
He doubted it and then began to sink.

He cried, "Lord, save me!" and Christ pulled him out.
"O man of little faith, why did you doubt?"

Once they got in the boat, winds instantly died down.
They knew not how Christ gave out bread or did not drown.

Those in the boat kneeled, each and every one,
In praise of Him, "You truly are God's Son."

105 Healings at Gennesaret
Mt. 14:34-36, Mk. 6:53-56, Jn. 6:22-25

After they crossed the Sea and made it to the shore,
The crowds flocked Him as they had done the day before.

They knew only one boat, sans Christ, set sail,
And waited for Him there, to no avail.

On realizing that Christ was not around,
They crossed the Sea and there Jesus was found.

From all around, they brought to Christ their ill,
For He could every wish of theirs fulfill

If they were able to His garment touch.
Christ gave to those who had in faith so much.

106 The Bread of Life
Jn. 6:26-59

Then Jesus asked, "Why is it I'm the One you seek?
For signs that filled your eye or bread that filled your cheek?

Don't labor for a bread that soon will perish,
But bread that gives the life that men shall cherish."

"What works, then, must we do, the Lord to please?"
"Believing He whom God sent will appease."

"What sign have You to show that should make us believe?
With manna did Moses their appetite relieve.

"But Moses never did a bread provide.
Were it for him alone, they'd all have died.

My Father gives you true heavenly bread,
That which gives life unto a world that's dead."

"Give us this bread, that we might always eat of it."
"I am the bread that does eternal life emit.

For he who comes to Me, his hunger I'll relieve,
Nor will he thirst, whoever does in Me believe.

I've told you, though you see Me, your faith's lacking.
No one the Father sends Me I'd send packing.

I have been heaven-sent, and do not My own will,
But all My Father wants in Me He did instill,

That I lose nothing that to Me was given,
But on the last day, with Me, it be risen.

He wills that those who see Me and believe
Shall meet their Maker, never for to leave,

That I should raise them on the final day."
Now Jews complained that these things Christ would say.

"He cannot claim to be from God descending.
We know His parents: He must be pretending."

"You men complain whereas you should repent.
None come to Me save by the Father sent,

Whom I shall raise up on the final day.
It's written, 'They'll learn what their God will say.'

Who from the Father learns will come to Me.

[156]

Now no one ever did the Father see,

Save He who from the Father has His being,
Who left heaven where Yahweh He was seeing.

He who believes receives the life eternal.
For he who has that hunger most internal,

I am the bread of life. For those who ate
With Moses did their pain alleviate,

But knew manna could not their death prevent,
As can the bread from Me, that's heaven-sent.

I am the living bread come down from heaven,
The bread that rises never needing leaven. [115]

Now everyone shall also rise, who eats this bread:
The bread that is My flesh will animate the dead."

The Jews argued, "How can He give His flesh to eat?"
"Lest you've My blood and flesh like it were wine and wheat, [115]

You shall as lifeless as a desert be. [115]
Yet those who eat shall rise and live with Me.

For My flesh is real food, My blood real drink.
As ships will do with water when they sink, [115]

They who consume Me, I shall live in them
And they shall live in Me. Carpe panem![116]

He gave Me life, Who sent Me here to dwell.
Those who eat Me draw life from Me as well.

For manna and the bread I give are not the same,
For Mine burns like the sun, the other a brief flame."

[157]

107 Many Disciples Take Offense at Jesus
Jn. 6:60-65

Now many in the synagogue protested,
"How can men tolerate what He suggested?!"

Since they complained at what they did not comprehend,
He asked, "What if you saw the Son of Man ascend

Back to the place from which He lived before?
The spirit, not the flesh, makes life outpour.

The words I speak to you are life and spirit,
Spoken to animate all those who hear it.

But there are some of you who don't believe."
For Christ knew to the darkness one would leave.

"That's why I said none come save by the Father's gift."
Then many followers forever went adrift.

108 "You Have the Words of Life Eternal"
Jn. 6:66-71

He asked the twelve, "You wish to go as well?"
Said Peter, "We'd leave heaven for what hell?

Who would we go to if from You we were to leave?
You have the words of life eternal, we believe,

And that You are God's Holy One, we've come to know.
We're here to stay, my Lord, and never shall we go."

"Did I not choose you twelve to be My own?
Yet one is evil, with a heart of stone."

From his foreknowledge these things Jesus said,
For one would take a payment for His head.

109 Defilement – Traditional and Real
Mt. 15:1-20, Mk. 7:1-23

There came a crowd of scribe and Pharisees
Exposing what they thought would God displease,

For His disciples ate with unwashed hands,
A crime that any good scribe reprimands.

(Jews wash, returning from the marketplace,
And many other customs they embrace.)

"Why do Your followers break the tradition
Of washing first? Why is there this omission?"

"Tell Me why you the Law of God transgress
In order to your own traditions bless.

It says 'Your parents you must honor and obey.'[117]
'Who speaks ill of them, let that be his final day.'[118]

Yet you say, 'What to God is dedicated
Need not go to those to whom you're related.'

So this way not a thing is sacrificed!
Were obligations e'er so cheaply priced?!?[119]

In letting men their obligations just avoid,
You've tried to make the Law that God has given void!

What did Isaiah say about the hypocrite?
'Though praise for Me these people from their lips emit,

[160]

Their hearts from Me are very separated,
As the precepts of men they've legislated.

The worship that they give Me is in vain.'[120]
You toss the Law so your customs remain.

What enters can't defile, without a doubt,
But what defiles a mouth is what comes out."

Disciples asked, not knowing how He should be read,
"Know you the Pharisees were hurt by what You said?"

"Regardless what's insulting or disputed,
What God has planted not will be uprooted.

Leave them alone, for they are mere blind guides,
Where he who leads into a tree collides,[121]

And stumbles backwards, dropping both in a ravine.
This fate befalls all led by those who have not seen."

"Explain how only things that leave defile."
"Well, food all travels south, unlike the Nile,[122]

Into the stomach and you all know how it leaves.
Yet what comes from the mouth shows what the heart believes."

(This way did Christ declare all foods are clean.)[123]
"From heart to mouth comes everything obscene,

The evil thoughts that lead to fornication,
Adultery, deceit, and defamation,

Licentiousness, folly, envy and pride,
Theft, murder, avarice and fratricide.

Men's vices, not traditions, must be banned,
So worry not who eats with unwashed hand."

110 The Syrophoenician Woman
Mt. 15:21-28, Mk. 7:24-30

Then Jesus went from there and, for a while,
Stayed at Sidon and Tyre, a land gentile.

As He entered a house, not wanting to be seen,
A local woman cried, "A demon most unclean

Has my girl in the most severe possession!
Lord, Son of David, please grant this concession!"

Christ did not answer. His disciples were annoyed,
"Send her away, that her loud cries we might avoid."

"I'm sent for the lost sheep of Israel."
She kneeled at Him, "Please make my daughter well."

"It's only fair that first the children should be fed;
It's wrong to throw to little dogs the children's bread."

"While this is true, still any dog is able
To feast on all that falls down from the table."

"You have great faith in My ability,
With boldness matched by your humility.[124]

In truth, when people do not have faith, hope, and love,
They're more like savage beasts than their Father above.

You only kiss the sky when, like a dog, you've kneeled. [125]
You need not worry, for your daughter I have healed."

She thankfully left Him for home and found
Her daughter healed, not by a demon bound.

111 Jesus Heals a Deaf Mute and Many Others
Mt. 15:29-31, Mk. 7:31-37

From there, He passed the Sea of Galilee
And climbed a mountain, where crowds came to see

Him heal the maimed, the blind, the dumb and lame.
And each of them a healed person became.

They brought a deaf man who had problems speaking:
That Christ lay hands on him his kin were seeking.

Christ then brought him aside, far from the multitude,
For to perform this miracle in solitude.

Christ put His finger in the deaf man's ear
And spat and touched his tongue and, being near,

He looked up to the heavens as He cried,
"Ephphatha!"[126] And, as told, ears opened wide,

While from his speech impediment he was released,
And spoke till all thought that his tongue could not be ceased.

Christ charged, "Do not this miracle proclaim."
Yet all the more His works just grew in fame.

They wondered how a man had such control,
That blind could see, dumb speak, and maimed made whole.

The lame could even walk. This left them so amazed
They looked up to the heavens, knelt and Yahweh praised.

112 Four Thousand are Fed
Mt. 15:32-39, Mk. 8:1-10

Days later, when the crowd came back around,
Christ knew that food for them could not be found.

He told His followers, "I feel such pity:
They've traveled through many a town and city,

And listened to Me, now, for three long days.
Although raised pagan, they gave Yahweh praise.

I'll not send them away, lest they should faint."
"If you did that, who could make a complaint?

With seven loaves, how could we feed so many?
Could one purchase a boat with just a penny?[127]

No easier could these loaves and three fish
Feed four thousand, no matter what You wish."

Then Jesus had the crowds sit on the ground.
Before He had them pass the loaves around,

Most grateful words to His father were spoken
And then He took the loaves and they were broken.

Likewise, He took the fish and they were blessed
And passed so that four thousand might ingest.

And eat is what they did, and did not stop until
They were so full that they could seven baskets fill.

Soon after this, Christ sent the crowds away
And went, himself, to Magadan to stay.

113 The Pharisees Seek a Sign
Mt. 16:1-4, Mk. 8:11-13

The Pharisees and Sadducees came by to test,
"Show us a sign from heaven and we'll be impressed."

"You know, seeing the sky, that it's a warning
That storms approach, with red skies in the morning.

Likewise, red skies, when seen before it's night,
Show you the weather will be just all right.

A rising western cloud foretells a shower
And south winds show heat will water devour.

You hypocrites interpret earth and sky;
Yet signs of present times just pass you by.

An evil generation seeks a sign,
But only that of Jonah shall be Mine."

He left the crowd of scribe and Pharisee
Sailing across the Sea of Galilee.

114 The Leaven of the Pharisees
Mt. 16:5-12, Mk. 8:14-21

Across the lake, his followers lacked bread,
Remembering just one loaf, so Christ said,

"The leaven of the Pharisees and Sadducees
Beware, for it is made from bold hypocrisies."

They told each other, "We've bread from no source."
"My friends, I did not mean that bread, of course.

Why are the words I speak to you not clear?
With ears of faith why can you all not hear?

Can't your eyes see? Or your hearts understand?
Did you forget I met their great demand

With short supplies, and baskets full remained?
Why is it when I speak your minds are strained?

115 A Blind Man is Healed at Bethesda
Mk. 8:22-26

Arriving at Bethesda, Christ was brought
A man who could not see and vision sought.

So Jesus took him from the crowds, outside
The village where saliva He applied,

Laid hands on him and asked him, "Can you see a thing?"
"I think so, but men look like trees whose branches swing."

So Jesus laid His hands on him again
And, instantly, the man saw men as men.

So Christ sent him away, back to his home,
Saying "Do not now through that village roam."

Chapter VII
The Way of the Cross

116 "You are the Christ, the Son of the Living God"
Mt. 16:13-20, Mk. 8:27-30, Lk. 9:18-21

Coming to Caesarea Philippi,
He asked, "According to men, who am I?"

Disciples answered, "Some say John has risen
After Herod beheaded him in prison,

While others say a prophet from of old."
"Do you think something else, or what you're told?"

Said Peter, "You're the Christ, the Lord's true Son."
"Simon Bar-Jona, you're a blessed one,

For not by flesh and blood was this revealed,
But God, by whom the truth is not concealed.

I tell you you are Cephas; on this rock
I'll build My Church and give it such a lock

The powers of hell could never overtake it.
I'll give the keys to heaven. If you make it

Bound on earth, then in heaven, too, it will be bound.
It will be loosed above what you loose on the ground."

He charged that His disciples not go spread
News He was the Messiah, as He said.

117 The First Prophecy of Jesus' Passion
Mt. 16:21-23, Mk. 8:31-33, Lk. 9:22

Then Jesus warned the twelve about His mission,
"The Son must suffer much and, in addition,

By elders, scribes and chief priests be rejected,
And killed, but on the third day resurrected."

Then Peter took Him and rebuked His Lord,
"You can't! Such pain and loss we can't afford!"

Then Peter was corrected, "Satan, get behind!
You do not think like God, but as men are inclined."

118 "If Any Man would Come after Me..."
Mt. 16:24-28, Mk. 8:34-9:1, Lk. 9:23-27, Jn. 12:25

So Jesus told them all, "Those who will follow
Must take a cross up, one that is not hollow.

You must deny yourselves and, to the grave,
Be faithful that your own life you not save.

You'll lose your life if saving it you choose,
And save it if for Me your life you lose.

What gain you if the whole world you control,
While, doing this, for all time lose your soul?

What can a man be given in return
If he, for all eternity, will burn?

To all who treat Me like I cause them shame,
When they're before the Lord, I'll do the same."

119 "Where Two or Three are Gathered Together..."
Mt. 18:19-20

"I tell you what two or three have requested
Shall by My dear Father be manifested.

Where two or three assemble in My name,
Among them's present He whom they proclaim."

120 The Transfiguration
Mt. 17:1-9, Mk. 9:2-10, Lk. 9:28-36

When these events had passed, after about a week,
Christ took James, John, and Peter up a mountain peak.

The three lay there and heavy were with sleep,
While Christ became whiter than any sheep,

His clothes like none could bleach, for as the sun He shone,
And they awoke to see that they were not alone.

For Moses and Elijah next to Christ appeared
And Peter, being nervous, said something most weird,

"Lord, that we're here is both good and correct.
Let us for each of you a booth erect."

A voice from heaven called them from a cloud,
"Hear My beloved Son, of whom I'm proud."

On hearing this, the three men fell prostrate,
But Jesus said, "Fear not, but elevate."

As they were coming down the mountainside,
He charged them, "Don't report this till I've died

And, on the third day, rise up from the dead."
Not knowing what He meant, nothing was said.

121 The Coming of Elijah
Mt. 17:10-13, Mk. 9:11-13

The twelve asked, "Pharisees claim that Elijah
Must come again, preceding the Messiah."

"In truth, I tell you He already came,
And, just as he was hurt, they've done the same.

He came and yet they knew him not nor did attempt;
Likewise, the Son of Man must suffer their contempt."

Predicting this, He Scripture did invoke
And they knew it was John of whom He spoke.

122 Jesus Heals a Boy Possessed by a Spirit
Mt. 17:14-21, Mk. 9:14-29, Lk. 9:37-43a

On coming down the mount, they met a crowd,
Who, with the scribes, were arguing most loud.

When they saw Him, the people were amazed,
Approached and greeted him, with voices raised.

"What have you all been arguing about?"
"My son's demon your men could not cast out.

The spirit's epileptic, deaf, and dumb.
My son falls often, when he's overcome,

Falls into fire or water at my home.
He cries, convulses, from his mouth comes foam."

"O generation, faithless and perverse,
How long must I endure people averse

To faith? Bring him to Me." And, on his way,
Convulsions sent him into disarray.

"How long has he this suffering endured?"
"Since childhood. Why could he not be cured?"

"For those with faith, all can occur, all get relief."
"I do believe, my Lord, but help my unbelief!"

[175]

"You spirit, deaf and dumb, and meant to burn,
Come out of him and ne'er again return!"

It caused its last convulsions, loudly cried,
And left, so many thought the boy had died.

Yet Jesus took his hand and he arose.
Then, later, as the day drew to a close,

His twelve disciples asked, each having doubt,
"How come we could not cast this demon out?"

"Had you faith as a grain of mustard seed,
You'd give commands where mighty trees take heed:

'Uproot yourself and seek the sea,' and they'd obey.
And these cannot be driven lest you fast and pray."

123 The Second Prophecy of Jesus' Passion
Mt. 17:22-23, Mk. 9:30-32, Lk. 9:43b-45

Christ gathered with the twelve in Galilee,
Seeking to give them teaching privately,

"I shall be handed to the hands of men,
Be killed and buried in a tomb, but then

On the third day, in truth, I shall arise."
They grasped it not, as hidden from their eyes,

Nor did they question Jesus further lest
More warnings make them even more distressed.

124 Payment of the Temple Tax
Mt. 17:24-27

Now Peter met a man collecting Temple tax,
Who asked, "Do you pay it or is your teacher lax?"

"Of course I do," and when he went inside,
Before he could ask, Christ said, "You decide:

From whom do earthly kings their taxes levy,
Demands that often are to poor men heavy?

Do they collect from sons or foreign men?"
When he said, "Foreigners," Christ said, "Amen,

The sons then are exempt. Though not to be
The fall of those who pay it earnestly,

Go to the sea right now and cast a hook.
Inside the first fish you catch shall you look

And in his mouth a sheckle shall you find.
Use it to pay our two taxes combined."

[178]

125 True Greatness
Mt. 18:1-5, Mk. 9:33-37, Lk. 9:46-48

Now in Capernaum, fierce debate arose
About the greatest one that Jesus chose.

Perceiving what was in their hearts, Christ said,
"The servant of you all shall be the head."

He called and then before them placed a child,
He held the kid, looked at the twelve, and smiled,

 "Unless you turn and like a child become,
Salvation shall not e'er be your outcome.

For all the greatest in the kingdom of the Lord
Lower themselves like children for a son's reward.

Whoe'er receives a child in My name
Receives Me and My Father just the same.

Who does not for himself praise allocate
Is he among your company who's great."

126 The Strange Exorcist
Mt. 10:42, Mk. 09: 38-41, Lk. 9:49-50

"A man casting out demons we did see,
In your name, but not in our company,"

John told him, "So we told him he must cease."
"Do no such thing. Such people should increase.

Who casts out demons while invoking Me
Must be considered friend, not enemy.

Who does not counter us is on our side."

127 Temptation, Correction, and Forgiveness
Mt. 18:6-9, Mk. 9:42-50, Lk. 17:1-4

"Yet those who have transgressions glorified,

Who turned a little one to sinful ways
Shall in Gehenna burn for endless days.

He'd better be with millstones fastened round
His neck and in the depths of the sea drowned.

Although temptation surely must exist,
Woe be to those who the tempter assist.

When brothers sin, they have to be corrected,
But when they're sorry, must not be rejected.

And should he wrong you seven times a day,
Repenting each time, send him not away."

128 On Reproving One's Brother
Mt. 18:15-18

"Should you feel you have been wronged by a brother,
Confront him, but not in front of another.

Should he concede your point, you've won your brother back.
If not, return with witnesses so you don't lack

Just evidence. And then, if still ignored,
Inform the church that you've had such discord.

Should he ignore concerns of yours still, then,
Treat him as you would tax collecting men,

Or Gentiles. Truly, what you loose or bind
In heaven loosed or bound up shall you find."

129 On Reconciliation
Mt. 18:21-22

Then Peter questioned, "Lord, how many times
Must I forgive him, when my brother's crimes

Victimize me? As many times as seven?"
"Seventy times seven if you seek heaven."

130 The Parable of the Unforgiving Servant
Mt. 18:23-35

"God's kingdom's like a king who settles his accounts
With slaves in debt to him in various amounts.

One came who did ten thousand talents[128] owe.
No means to pay it back did this man know.

Unto him who could not control his greed,[129]
The master sat in judgment and decreed,

'Since you've no way of paying back your debt,
The penalty for this offense I've set:

You shall, with wife and kids and goods, be sold
As slaves, where you shall work until you're old.'

The servant, in despair, fell to his knees,
And begged his master, 'Lord, have patience, please!

I'll pay it all! Just grant me some more time!'
The king knew that this height he couldn't climb,

And let him down, forgiving all he owed,
Thus granting peace instead of the abode.

He thanked the king and got back on his feet.
He left and met a man while on the street,

[184]

A man who owed him a hundred denarii.
Although his fellow servant was so sorry,

He slapped the man and further did attack.
'I'll make you suffer till it's all paid back!'

Despite the other servant's desperate pleas,
Naught but full payment would this man appease.

When he was thrown in jail till all the debt was paid,
The first servant could not contain the news he made.

When other servants heard, they were distressed
And to the king, this news did they attest.

The king said, 'Because you've not mercy learned,
You'll rot in jail till your full debt's returned.'

The master had him handed over to
The torturers. So shall it be with you

Who will not with his heart his foe forgive.
In agony for all his days will live."

Chapter VIII
Last Journey to Jerusalem

131 Jesus Decides to Go to Jerusalem
Mt. 19:1-2, Mk. 10:1, Lk. 9:51

When He had finished up with all this teaching,
He traveled south and, all the way, was preaching.

Yet they knew, still, that Christ was leaving them,
Who had his face set towards Jerusalem.

132 Jesus is Rejected by Samaritans
Lk. 9:52-56

Before He reached Samaria, His men were sent,
But were not welcomed, knowing what was His intent.

Since Jesus was towards David's city bound,
No welcome in Samaria He found.

So James and John asked, "Should we bid that fire
From heaven consume them, as did Elijah?"

Then Christ rebuked them harshly, "You don't know
What spirit you are of, what your words show.

I came to save men's souls, not to destroy."
And so another road did they employ.

133 Commissioning the Seventy-Two[130]
Lk. 10:1-12

Then Jesus appointed seventy-two
To preach in places He would then go through.

He told them, sending them out two-by-two,
"The harvest is great, but laborers few.

Pray to the Lord more harvesters be sent."
And then He further warned before they went,

"I send you out as sheep with wolves surrounding,
So travel not with worldly goods abounding.

Don't carry bags for silver or for gold,
Nor shall you spare tunics or sandals hold,

Nor staff; for laborers deserve their food.
Don't greet men on the road, but don't be rude.

When someone welcomes you, stay in his place.
On entering, wish for that home God's grace.

Bestow your peace on them, if they deserve it,
And if they are unworthy, you'll conserve it.

[188]

When you are served, eat what's set at the table.
Make the sick healed and those who can't walk able.

Proclaim the kingdom: if they'll not receive you,
Shake their dust from your feet so when you leave, you

Show God how they lack hospitality.
Then they'll, for their great immorality,

Far worse than Sodom and Gomorrah burn,
Who made peace from my peacemakers return.

Tell that town, 'God's kingdom has met you here.
What you cast out shall fill your heart with fear.'"

134 Woes Pronounced on Galilean Cities
Mt. 11:20-24, Lk. 10:12-15

He then began the cities to condemn
Who had rejected what was done for them.

"Woe to you, Bethsaida and Chorazin,
Who've seen great works and yet still live in sin!

Had such been done in Sidon or in Tyre,
So desperately forgiveness they'd desire.

They'd be in ash and sackcloth long ago.
Compared to them, you shall have greater woe.

Capernaum, think you God is to exalt you?
Instead, you'll fall to hell, for God will fault you

For witnessing His works, but still not moving.
For men of Sodom would have been improving

On seeing such works done before their eyes.
One day, you'll more than Sodom agonize."

135 The Return of the Seventy-two
Lk. 10:17-20

The six dozen returned, rejoicing, "Lord,
Demons were slain with your name as our sword!"

Christ said, "I saw Satan like lightning fall,
From heaven to the ground, where serpents crawl.

Against serpents I've given you the power
To tread upon their heads. They'll not devour,

Nor cause you lasting harm in any way.
Do not rejoice that demons must obey,

But that because of virtue, faith, and love,
Your names shall be imprinted up above."

136 Jesus' Thanksgiving to the Father
Mt. 11:25-27, Lk. 10: 21-24

"I thank thee, Father, Lord of all the universe,
Who leaves the wise in darkness and makes babes well versed,

For such reversal was your gracious will.
He's filled My cup so it began to spill.

All things He gave, from Father to the Son.
For no one knows the Son except this One.

Except the Son, of course, no single person knows
His Father, except those revealed to, whom He chose."

137 The Lawyer's Question
Lk. 10:25-28

A lawyer came to Jesus for to test,
"What must I do to gain eternal rest?"

Christ said, "Well, what, my friend, is written in the Law?"
"Of all the words of God's therein I ever saw,

What I think is the most important part
Is 'Love the Lord, your God, with all your heart

And all your soul, and all your strength and mind,'
And, what I think with this is intertwined[131]

Is 'Love your neighbor as yourself.'" "You're right.
Do this and you shall always see the light."

This man, wanting himself to justify,
Said, "Who's my neighbor, just to clarify?"

138 The Parable of the Good Samaritan
Lk. 10:29-37

Christ taught, "A man went down to Jericho,
Where great hardship he came to undergo.

For bandits beat him, stripped him, and left him for dead.
And who would you think made the effort to bestead?

The first to pass this man by was a priest,[132]
Who should know best but acted as the least.

He passed on the other side of the road.
Soon after this, a Levite[132] likewise strode,

Avoiding contact from the other side.
Then a Samaritan walked right beside.

On seeing him thus, he was with such pity moved,
He did all possible to see his health improved.

For after all the victim's wounds were treated,
His act of love was still not yet completed.

He brought the man, on donkey, to an inn,
And cared for him, as one would do for kin.

He left the innkeeper with two denarii,
And told the man, 'Look, sir, I'm really sorry

That I must leave. Use this to heal my friend.
I'll reimburse you after my trip's end

Should it not cover the entire cost.'"
The question was back at the lawyer tossed,

 "Which of these three men acted like a neighbor?"
"The third." "Then thus you must for others labor."

139 Mary and Martha[133]
Lk. 10:38-42

While entering a village, on their way,
Christ met with Martha and she bid them stay.

Her sister, Mary, sat at her Lord's feet
And gave to Him her focus most complete.

So busy serving her guests and her Lord,
Some help from Jesus Martha then implored,

"Do you not care for what You must observe,
That Mary's doing nothing while I serve?

Please have her help me." Yet Jesus refused.
"She is not lazy; rather, you're confused.

For, as you serve guests, you stress out, you hurry,
And many things there are that make you worry.

Few things are needed, just one thing required.
Her choice shall not be taken, but admired."

140 The Persistent Friend at Midnight
Lk. 11:5-8

He asked them, "Which of you who has a friend,
And goes at midnight, asking, 'Will you lend

Three loaves to me, because a friend of mine
Arrived and we've nothing on which to dine?'

Would hear from him, 'Be gone and ask no more!
It's late, we sleep, and locked shut is my door!

I cannot give a thing.'? He would instead
Get up, though late, and give his friend some bread.

If not for friendship, then for his insistence
Would he get up and give his friend assistance."

141 Jesus is Accused of Being Possessed
Mt. 12:22-30, Mk. 3:22-27, Lk. 11:14-23

They brought to Christ a man both dumb and blind,
"Please heal him with such handicaps combined,

For by a mighty demon he's possessed
And many here to Your great works attest."

Christ healed the man, who then both spoke and saw.
And, seeing this, the people were in awe.

"Can power like this come from David's Son?"
But Pharisees said, "Nay, the other one.

He's from Beelzebul, the prince in Satan's land.
No other means allow one to demons command."

He knew their hearts and minds and so He chided,
"A kingdom that's against itself divided

Will crumble like a castle build on sand. [134]
No city set against itself can stand.

Should Satan aid those casting out his demons
He might as well start war within his legions.

If I'm evil for casting demons out,
What are your sons, who do the same, about?

[198]

Hence shall these sons be judges over you.
And if, through God, do I demons subdue,

God's kingdom's warriors have come here attacking.
To rob a strong man, one thing can't be lacking.

He must be bound so he has no defenses
Or else beware the painful consequences.

Once overcome, one may his riches plunder
And I have come to tear his house asunder.

All those who are not with Myself allied
Will perish fighting for the other side.

In truth I say, all men with Me will gather
Or else shall they like crowds in rainfall[135] scatter."

142 The Sin Against the Holy Spirit
Mt. 12:31-32, Mk. 3:28-30, Lk. 12:10

"I tell you every sin and blasphemy
Can pardoned be, even affronts to Me,

Save who against the Holy Spirit will blaspheme.
Such false transgressions nothing ever can redeem.

I must repeat forgiveness won't be seen.
They said 'He has a spirit most unclean.'

We judge the goodness of trees by their fruit.
My works are good so don't condemn My root.

You brood of vipers! What know you of good?!
You're as much evil as a tree is wood![136]

A good man's mouth will give forth treasures while

From yours spews hatred, blasphemy, and bile![1]

On judgment day, you must render account
For bad words spoken in any amount.

For some people, their words shall justify,
While others for the words they said shall fry."

143 The Return of the Evil Spirit
Mt. 12:43-45, Lk. 11:24-26

"When unclean spirits do a person leave,
They go through dry wastelands seeking reprieve.

They find no rest no matter where they roam
And say, 'I'll go back to my former home.'

Arriving, finding it unoccupied,
He'll come, with seven others, to reside,

With each of them more evil than the first,
Leaving the victim ever more accursed.

Be wary of them if you seek salvation
For such shall happen to this generation."

144 True Blessedness
Lk. 11:27-28

A woman then called from the crowd, "How truly blest
Are both the womb that bore you and your mother's breast!"

But Christ responded, "Rather, blest are they
Who hear My word and keep it everyday."

145 The Sign of Jonah
Mt. 12:38-42, Lk. 11:16, 29-32

Then Christ was asked by scribes and Pharisees,
"Hey, teacher, show us a sign, if you please."

 "A generation that's adulterous
And evil seeks a sign. You must not miss

The only sign you ever shall be shown,
The sign of Jonah. I shall lay in stone,

As he was in the belly of a whale,
Three days and nights, and yet I will prevail.

As Ninevites harkened to Jonah's sign,
This generation best take heed from Mine.

The Ninevites shall rise on Judgment Day
Condemning who in sinful ways did stay.

For, as they heard a prophet and repented,
Your lack of changing has your fate cemented.

Likewise, the queen of the South[137] shall arise,
Who went far to hear Solomon the Wise,

Condemning your deaf ears with words severe,
For one greater than Solomon is here.

146 On True Vice and Virtue
Lk. 11:37-41

Christ finished speaking when a Pharisee
Asked Him, "Will You not come and dine with me?"

So Christ accepted, "Sure, that would be grand."
But sitting down, He ate with unwashed hand.

This breech of custom made those there astonished.
Christ spoke up so He could not be admonished.

 "You clean the outside of the dish and chalice,
While you are filled with extortion and malice.

You fools! Who made the skin made everything between.
Give alms from what you have and all for you is clean."

147 Warning against Avarice
Lk. 12:13-15

A member of the crowd cried, "Master, please demand
My brother share inherited riches and land!"

 "Who made Me your own judge and arbitrator?"
Then, to the crowds, "Be no accumulator,

For who lives for possessions has much less,
Even if riches add up to excess."

148 The Parable of the Rich Fool
Lk. 12:16-21

Christ taught, "A rich man had such fertile land
Its yield was greater than he ever planned.

He said, 'I've not room for my crops to store.
What shall I do? I know! Since I want more,

I'll tear my barn down, build a giant one
And be the envy of near everyone.

For there I'll store my grain and all I own
And then I'll say unto myself alone,[138]

"My soul, you're saved up for many a year
So just relax, eat, drink, be of good cheer!"'

But God will say to him, 'You fool! This night
Your life will end and, as you lack foresight,

You can't take with you anything you stored.'
For those who are not rich towards the Lord

And make pleasure and wealth their biggest goal
Will wallets have as empty as their soul."

[206]

149 The Parable of the Barren Fig Tree
Lk. 13:1-9

There were some present at that very time
Who told the Christ of Pilate's gruesome crime.

They asked why Galileans paid that price:
Their blood was mingled with their sacrifice.

Christ asked, "Do you think they sinned worse than others,
Just punishment undeserved by their brothers?

I tell you that, unless you all repent,
There's far worse hell to which you will be sent.

Were those on whom the Siloam tower fell
More than their neighbors on their way to hell?

You must repent and listen to My instruction.
You must believe you're on the eve of destruction.[139]

A man once had a fig tree in his yard,
Which was not held in very high regard,

For every time he came seeking a fig
He found the branches just grew leaf and twig.

He told his worker, 'For three years I found
Not one fig here. Why should it waste the ground?'

 'This fig tree's fruitlessness I realize,
But let me dig around and fertilize

Before I cut it down. Give me a year.
If there's no fruit, we'll get it out of here.

For how great would it be if fruit would grow?
There are few better tastes on earth I know.'"

150 The Healing of the Crippled Woman on the Sabbath
Lk. 13:10-17

One Sabbath in the synagogue He taught,
When someone crippled eighteen years was brought.

She was so bent, so decreased was her height:
This demon had not let her stand upright.

On seeing her, He said, "You're freed from your disease."
Once Christ laid hands on her, she walked upright with ease.

She praised God that she was no longer bent.
But, in the synagogue, the president

Was furious about this Sabbath healing.
So he was to all those gathered appealing,

"Six days are made for work and one for rest!
Come on those six if healing's your request."

"You hypocrites, who follow no such rule!
Would you leave tied up donkey, ox, or mule?

Would you towards water lead the beast away,
Or leave it thus, to keep the Sabbath day?

What decent man would leave beasts in a manger?
And if one can't leave animals in danger,

How much more pressing than a drink of water,
Is Satan's binding up Abraham's daughter?

With her bound eighteen years, think you I should
Wait one more day before I do this good?

Think you the Sabbath is kept in this way?
By giving Satan power one more day?!"

As He said this, His enemies were put to shame
And crowds rejoiced and glorified Jesus' name.

151 Herod the Fox
Lk. 13:31-33

At that time, Pharisees came by and said,
"Get far from here, for Herod wants you dead!"[140]

 "Go tell that fox that I cast demons out
Two days and, on the third, complete my route.

Regardless of this all, as for Myself today,
Tomorrow, and the next, I must be on My way.

For prophets must travel to David's city
And feel the wrath of men who have no pity."

152 The Healing of the Man with Dropsy
Lk. 14:1-6

One Sabbath, Christ dined with a Pharisee,
Where eyes were fixed on Jesus constantly.

A man with dropsy then was brought before Him.
He asked, "Should Sabbath law make Me ignore him?"

Then neither Pharisees nor lawyers spoke.
As if the man had ne'er before awoke,

He felt refreshed as Jesus gave him healing.
Christ asked, "What man could e'er be so unfeeling,

To let a son or ox just in a deep well lie
To follow Sabbath law?" To this they'd no reply.

153 Teaching on Humility and Places of Honor
Lk. 14:7-14

Then Jesus taught a parable to show each guest,
For they had each sought out the seat that was the best.

"When you're invited to a wedding feast,
It better is to seek the seat that's least.

If you should take a seat of honor, as men strive,
What then, if men of greater honor might arrive?

You'd be ashamed, then, going to a lower place.
How would you leave a seat of honor and save face?

The wiser man knows that he should be meek,
And that a guest the lowest seat should seek.

Your host may then say, 'Good friend, move up higher!
A place of honor your name does require.'

Then all shall see you honored, not ashamed.
The proud shall be denounced; the meek acclaimed.

When hosting dinners, you should not invite
Friends, brothers, or rich neighbors, all who might

Return the favor and leave you repaid.
Invite the poor, the blind, all who need aid.

Since they cannot repayment e'er afford,
The blessings from above will be outpoured."

154 The Parable of the Lost Sheep
Mt. 18:12-14, Lk. 15:1-7

The Pharisees came by for to chagrin,
And said, "This man breaks bread with those who sin."

So He reached out to those who were so lost,
"You all know just how much one sheep can cost.

When one sheep of a hundred goes away,
Who with the faithful ninety-nine would stay?

Instead, you'd leave the ninety-nine behind,
And when the sheep who'd lost his way you find,

You would rejoice and lay it on your back,
Unless love, joy, or gratitude you lack.

Once home, you'd gather the community
To celebrate and share your joie de vie.

Just so, in heaven will there be much joy
Whenever sinners will virtue employ

And turn back to their God, more so than when
The ninety-nine remain as faithful men."

155 The Parable of the Lost Coin
Lk. 15:8-10

"What woman with ten coins, if one were lost,
Would not search everything, and spare no cost?

When found, she'd gather those who have her love,
To sing, 'Give praise and thanks to God above!'

Likewise, when one is lost, the Lord laments
And celebrates when one sinner repents."

156 The Parable of the Prodigal Son
Lk. 15:11-32

Christ taught, "There was a man who two sons had.
The younger one said to his father, 'Dad,

I want to get my half. I want it now.
So every other calf and goat and cow

And half your lands should come to me, your son.'
And, just as he requested, it was done.

He sold it all and left his home behind
To squander it on sins of every kind.

When all was spent, on women, dice, and wine,[141]
The grapes had withered up, without their vine.[142]

This distant land was by a famine struck.
This foolish son found he was out of luck.

He found himself a job where pigs he'd feed.
They paid so low that so great was his need

He gladly would have eaten what pigs ate,
But no one would his pain alleviate.

He finally woke up. 'How dumb I've been!
I'll tell my father how great was my sin

Against him and his mercy I'll implore.
My father's servants have their fill and more,

While here I starve. I'll leave this place and then
Beg Father, "Treat me like your hired men!

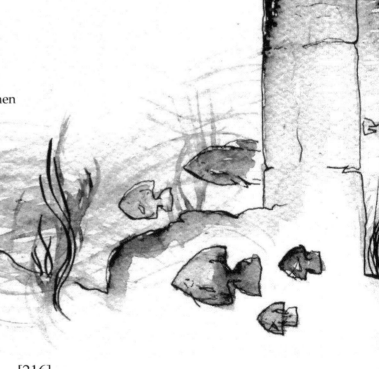

My sin is so great; call me not your son!
I beg forgiveness though I merit none."'

Still far from home, his father saw his boy,
And, filled with pity, overcome by joy,

Ran to his son, and hugged and kissed him, too.
The son said, 'Father, I've sinned against you

And heaven. Please, just treat me as a slave.'
'When you returned, my old heart you did save.

Garçon![143] My finest robe, please, will you bring?
Get sandals for his feet! And get a ring!

Our fatted calf, too, I would have you kill.
We'll celebrate till all have had their fill!

My son was dead, but came up from the ground!
My little boy was lost, but now is found.'

They then began to sing and dance and play.
The older son was out working all day.

He heard the song and dance as he drew near,
And called one of the servants, 'Hey! Come here!

What all this is about I've not yet learned.'
'Your brother, who was gone, has now returned!

Your father, who was mourning, was so thrilled
He took the fatted calf and had it killed.'

The angry son stayed outside and did pout.
The father heard of this and so went out

And urged his son to join in, but was told,
'For all these years, I've been as good as gold.

Not one order of yours I've disobeyed,
And how, for slavery, am I repaid?

Never one single goat to share with friends!
Yet he whose greed and lust just never ends

Receives the fatted calf, that son of yours
Who spent his whole birthright on wine and whores!'

'Dear son, I always have you here with me.
All that I own we share communally

And when I go, then you shall have it all.
One must rejoice when good news does befall.

You say that I do not share equally
While you'll not let me share my joie de vie,

For your dead brother came up from the ground!
The one who was so lost, he now is found!'"

157 The Parable of the Shrewd Steward
Lk. 16:1-9

Christ taught, "A rich man had a steward who
Was found dishonest. Once the master knew,

He called this wasteful steward for to scold,
'What's all of this of which I have been told?

Draw an account up of your stewardship,
For from you your position I will strip.'

He said unto himself, 'What shall I do?
How I should earn a living I've no clue.

I lack the strength that one would need to dig.
To beg I'd feel as shameful as a pig.

Ah, I know what I'll do, while time remains.
I'll make some friends by sacrificing gains.

They might into their homes then welcome me.
He called his master's debtor's in to see,

'How much, good sir, do you my master owe?
For you my own commission I'll forego.'

'A hundred measures of oil,' the first said.
'Here, take your bond. Write fifty down instead.'

'And I owe a hundred measures of wheat.'
'Write eighty and I'll call the debt complete.'

The master praised him, then, for being clever.[144]
In life, such giving gains rewards forever.

In things financial, children of the light
Are less astute than those with worldly sight.

For money, often used to evil ends,
Should be dispersed to gain eternal friends.

For then, when you face judgment, when you die,
Your life of virtue they will verify

And welcome you into the kingdom of the Lord."

158 On Faithfulness in What is Least
Lk. 16:10-12

"If folks know trust in you they always can afford,

You would be trustworthy with treasures great.
Those crooked with small things possess the trait

In all things, great and small. If you misuse
Your wealth, and on yourself you always choose

To spend this tainted thing, you'll not deserve
Eternal wealth, since you had failed to serve

Your master well. If you can't trusted be,
With things that are not yours ultimately,

Who will give you what is your very own?"

159 On Serving Two Masters
Lk. 16:13

"A subject only bows before one throne.

No slave can serve two masters. If he tried,
You know exactly what would soon betide.

He'd love the second master and he'd hate the first,
Or vice versa. Of all servants, he'd be the worst.

One can't to God and money be a slave.
One master would condemn while one would save."

160 The Pharisees Rebuked
Lk. 16:14-15

The Pharisees, who deeply loved gold, then did jeer.
Christ said, "You act so holy, as if God you fear.

God knows your hearts, though men think you're upright.
What men will praise is hated in God's sight."

161 The Endurance of the Law
Lk. 16:16-17

"'Till John the Baptist's time, it was the Law
And prophets that the people heard and saw.

From then onwards, the kingdom of the Lord's been preached.
Folks try to storm it, but the wall has not been breached.

Sooner would earth and heaven be destroyed
Than one drop of the Law be null and void."

162 Concerning Divorce
Lk. 16:18

"As one can't serve wealth here and God above,
In life only one woman can you love.

As love of money surely is idolatry,[145]
Divorce and then remarriage is adultery.

Men, know, besides this sin when you're divorced,
Your wife into a life of sin is forced.

Don't marry someone who's their marriage ended,
For wounds are meant to heal and tears be mended."

163 The Parable of the Rich Man and Lazarus
Lk. 16:19-31

There was a rich man who was so well dressed
His clothes and daily feasts made all impressed.

Yet, at his gate, there was a man so poor
He begged to eat what fell upon the floor.

This Lazarus appeared so sad and sick
That dogs came by just for his sores to lick.

From hunger then the poor man passed away
And he was brought to Abraham to stay

Forever with his God and his forefather.
And so died, too, the man who wouldn't bother

To feed this Lazarus. To hell he went,
Where looking up above from his torment,

He saw the two and called up, 'Father, please!
Send Lazarus my sufferings to ease!

Have sympathy. Let him just wet his finger
To cool my tongue. In agony I linger.'

'On earth, you lacked one drop of agape,
So thirsty, unextinguished you must stay.

In life, you had much more than you could need
And you would not your starving brother feed.

Your states have changed; this cannot altered be.
Besides, a chasm divides you and he,

Preventing those who would from one side cross.'
'Then, Abraham, if you can't save my loss,

Send Lazarus unto my brothers five,
Who can be saved while they are still alive.'

'But prophets were already to them sent.'
'If one came from the dead, they would repent.'

'They listened not to what the prophets said,
They'd still not hear should one rise from the dead.'"

164 The Blessings and Woes[146]
Lk. 6:20b-23

"Blest are you poor, for in God's kingdom you'll reside.
Blest are you hungry, for you shall be satisfied.

Blest are you sorrowful, for you shall laugh,
And most blest are you if, on My behalf,

You're driven out, detested, and abused,
With all harsh words in your direction used.

Rejoice that day, and leap in exultation.
Who has a prophet's hardship shares his station.

Woe to you rich, who shall be always poor,
While those who laugh and sneer smile no more.

Great woe to those whose daily supper is a feast,
Who shall know hunger pains of those who have the least.

And woe to you when nice things people say,
For false prophets were treated in this way.

165 We are Unprofitable Servants
Lk. 17:7-10

"What man, whose servant has been minding sheep,
And then returns, asks him, 'Do you need sleep?

Or would you rather just recline at table?'
Would he not rather say, for he is able,

'Make tight your belt and serve to me my food;
Then you can eat.' Need he show gratitude

Because his servant did as he was told?
When you've done well, don't act like you are gold.

Say 'I'm a servant, one of little use.
No more than what's required I produce.'"

166 The Cleansing of the Ten Lepers
Lk. 17:11-19

While towards Jerusalem, Jesus did see,
Between Samaria and Galilee,

Ten lepers who were standing far away.
"Please, Jesus, Master, pity us, we pray!"

He told them, "Go and show yourselves before the priest."
And on their way, from their disease they were released.

One saw this, ran back and, with his voice raised,
Fell on his face at Christ and Yahweh praised.

Christ asked, "Did I heal one leper or ten?
What happened to those nine ungrateful men?

Could just this foreigner return and thank the Lord?
Rise up and leave, your faith has made your health restored."

167 On the Coming of the Kingdom of God
Lk. 17:20-21

Then Pharisees asked, "When will God's kingdom appear?"
Christ said to them, "No sign shall show the end is near.

No one shall say, 'The end is here!' 'It's there!'
The kingdom's here, though you are not aware."

168 The Parable of the Unjust Judge
Lk. 18:1-8

Christ taught this for persistence to impart,
"When praying, don't give up or e'er lose heart.

A judge once feared not God and loved not men.
A widow sought him again and again,

Who rightly sought from him some vindication.
He said, 'She even comes on my vacation![147]

Though I've refused and care not what is right,
What I'd not do to get her from my sight!

I'll do it not from moral obligation,
But fear of harm to self or reputation.'"

Christ said, "You see how rules the unjust judge.
How quicker would your Father be to budge?

Though you may find this justice oft delayed,
Be sure, in time, that all is fully paid.

I promise you that those who always pray
Unto their God, persistent night and day

Will get a thousand times more than is fair.
When Christ comes, will He find faith anywhere?"

169 The Pharisee and the Publican
Lk. 18:9-14

He spoke to those who thought themselves so pure,
As if, in their goodness, they were secure.

 "Two men went out to temple separately,
A tax collector and a Pharisee.

The Pharisee knelt down there to condemn,
'Thanks, Lord, for making me so unlike them,

Unjust committers of adultery.
This tax collector is so unlike me.

I fast twice weekly, tithes I always pay.'
The tax collector stood there, far away,

Not daring to his eyes to heaven raise,
'Lord, save this sinner from the fiery blaze!'

He beat his breast, and 'Mea culpa!'[148] cried.
This man, and not the first, left justified.

For those who raise themselves will be knocked down,
While humble folk will win themselves renown."

Chapter IX
Jesus at the Feast of
Tabernacles in Jerusalem

170 Jesus Remains in Galilee
Jn. 7:1-9

Then Jesus went about in Galilee,
For in Judea, scribe and Pharisee

Sought to kill Him, though it was not His time,
For at another feast they'd do their crime.

The feast of Shelters[149] of the Jews drew near
And his brothers said, "Get away from here,

Down to Judea. Your disciples there
Could see Your works and crowds could be aware.

None act in secret for to be known publicly,
But in Jerusalem the world could Your works see."

For even His own kin did not believe.
"The right time has not come for Me to leave,

Although, for you, most any time is fine.
The world hates Me but is, to you, benign

Because I testify about its evil ways.
Go to the festival and give to Yahweh praise.

But, as for Me, the time is not ripe yet."
Christ stayed behind, till sun was nearly set.

171 Journey to Jerusalem in Secret
Jn. 7:10-13

Then, later on, He went there, secretly,
Where Jews looked for Him, asking, "Where is He?"

About the Christ those there had much discourse:
"He's good." "No, He leads men on the wrong course."

To speak their minds, though, loudly, few would choose,
All out of fear of leaders of the Jews.[150]

172 Teaching in the Temple
Jn. 7:14-39

Midway into the feast, Christ in the Temple taught,
A challenge to all those who Jesus' life sought.

The Jews were shocked and asked, "How can He read?
Lacking a teacher should this goal impede."

"The teachings that I give do not from My heart flow,
But from the One who willed that I to earth should go.

Those who will do what is commanded by the Lord
Know if I teach for God or of My own accord.

When someone on his own account will speak,
It is because glory and fame they seek.

He who says someone else has honor due
Has not corruption and his words are true.

For Moses gave the Law that you all break,
But tell Me why you wish My life to take."

They said, "Who wants You dead? You are insane!"
"One work I did won wonder and disdain.

For Moses ordered that you circumcise,
(Though it was done before him). All advise

That it must be done on your son's eighth day alive.
The seventh day[151] should not this healing work deprive.

If Sabbath work can just one member heal,
Should I not cure the whole of its ordeal?

[236]

You must not judge by how a thing appears,
But how to what is just the thing adheres."

Some people from Jerusalem then said,
"Is not Jesus the man who they want dead,

Here speaking freely and they've no reply?
Could they know He's the one sent from on high?

How is that, since we know His origin?
The Christ shall come and none know where He's been."[152]

He said, "You know Me and from whence I came.
Yet I'm not here for My glory and fame.

I do not come here of My own accord,
But I was sent here by a truthful Lord.

I know Him though you people know Him not,
By whom I both was sent here and begot."

The leaders wanted to arrest Him at this time,
But since His hour had not come, they did no crime.

Now, many in the crowd there did believe:
"Could the Messiah greater things achieve?"

At hearing crowds talk thus, the Pharisees
Told Temple guards that they must Jesus seize.

"For only a short time will I be with you still.
I shall return to whom My mission did instill.

You'll look for Me, but unable to find
And powerless to follow Me behind."

The Jews asked, "Where does He intend to go,
That we could neither follow, find, or know?

Will He set sail to teach among the Greeks?
What could He mean when this is what He speaks:

'You'll look for Me, but unable to find,
And powerless to follow Me behind.'?"

When came the final, great day of the feast,
Christ yelled, "Let those with thirst come see it ceased!

Let anyone with faith in Me come here and drink!
For 'living water, deep enough in which to sink,'

As Scripture says, 'shall flow out from his heart.'"[153]
He spoke then of the Spirit He'd impart,

The Spirit that He did not yet provide,
For Jesus had not yet been glorified.

173 Division among the People regarding Jesus
Jn. 7:40-52

Some there said, "He's the prophet," some "The Christ is He,"
Yet some asked, "Would the Christ come out of Galilee?

It's said His kingship is from David's line passed down,
And He shall come from Bethlehem, from David's town."

They disagreed, some wanted him arrested,
But none did as the chief priests had suggested.

The guards went to the priests and Pharisees,
Who asked them, "Why did you not Jesus seize?"

"No one has ever spoken like this man."
"So you've been led astray, into His clan?

Does any Pharisee believe Him? Any priest?
He knows no Law, which will condemn Him when deceased."

One of the Pharisees, named Nicodemus,[154]
Said, "Law forbids that you condemn this Jesus,

That is, until you first grant him a hearing,
To tell if He's transgressing or adhering."

"Are you a Galilean, too? You go and see.
We know prophets do not arise in Galilee."

174 The Woman Caught in Adultery[155]
Jn. 7:53–8:11

They went home and Christ to the Mount of Olives went.
At daybreak, He left for the Temple, as if sent.

A crowd there came to Him and they were taught,
While scribes and Pharisees a woman brought,

For she was caught adultery committing.
So they asked Him, "What punishment is fitting?

For she has been caught in the very act
And Moses told us how we should react,

That we should stone her. What is your command?"
They asked this, hoping they could reprimand

If Christ the Law of Moses contradicted,
From His compassion for all those afflicted.

To this, He started writing on the ground,
To their surprise, that they heard not a sound.

When they persisted, He stood, saying, "I concur.
Let he who has not sinned throw the first stone at her."

Christ wrote some more and each man dropped his stone,
The eldest first, till two were left alone.

The woman stayed, ashamed, while Christ rose to His feet.
He asked, "Do none remain to judge, stone or maltreat?"

"No, none, Lord. Gone are all those frightful men."
"You're pardoned. Go and do not sin again."

175 "I am the Light of the World"
Jn. 8:12-20

Now, later, came a crowd, and Jesus said,
"I am the light of the world. All those led

By Me won't walk in darkness, but life-giving light."
The Pharisees spoke, hoping that their words could smite,

"Your testimony is Your glory seeking.
That means You must not truthfully be speaking."

"Though on My own behalf I testify,
This does not My witness disqualify.

My testimony's true because I know
From whence I came and also where I'll go.

You neither know My roots nor destination.
By human standards comes your condemnation.

I do not judge, and even if I would,
It would be true and based on what is good.

I'm not alone, but with the One who sent Me,
Whose witness with My own is complementary.

The Law says what two witness to is true:
The Father testifies about Me, too."

They asked, assuming that His claims were phony,
"Where is your Father and His testimony?"

"You do not know Me, nor My kin, nor where We dwell.
If you knew Me, you would know My Father as well."

He spoke this where they kept the Temple treasure,
And though it caused the priests there much displeasure,

He was untouched because His hour was not yet.

176 Discussion with the Jews
Jn. 8:21-29

"You'll search, like men who look west for a sun that's set,[156]

When I have gone, and unable to find,
You'll die and with your sin be intertwined.

Where I go you can't follow or walk right beside."
They asked, "When He speaks thus, does He mean suicide?"

"You're from below, while I am from above.
I am not from the world you're from and love.

As I already told you, in your sins you'll fall;
Lest you believe that I am He, this will befall."

So they asked Him, "Who are You?" He replied,
"What answer did I this whole time provide?

I've much to judge of this world, much to say,
A message from My Father I relay."

They did not understand the person Jesus meant.
"You'll lift the Son of Man and make it evident

That I am He and work not of My own accord,
And My words I've learned from My Father and My Lord.

The One who sent Me left Me not alone,
For He is pleased by all the works I've shown."

177 "The Truth Shall Set You Free"
Jn. 8:30-36

While He spoke, many Jews came to believe.
So He said to the people, "If you leave

Where dwells your heart, and live inside My word,
You'll know what things are true and what absurd.

And, knowing this, you'll My disciples be.
From bondage, then, the truth shall set you free."

"We come from Abraham and none has been a slave,"
They challenged Jesus, "From what bondage will You save?"

"Men are mere slaves, all those who live in sin.
For slaves hold no position, as do kin.

A son's place can't cease in a family,
So if you are freed by the Son, you're free."

178 Children of the Devil
Jn. 8:37-47

"I know that you descend from Abraham,
But, as you think My words and claims a sham,

This makes you want to commit homicide.
What I speak I've heard at My Father's side.

In truth, you also do your father's will."
"Our Father's Abraham, we tell you still."

"If Abraham's blood in your heart was ample,
You'd live a life that follows his example.

For, as it is, you want to see Me dead,
But I've told you the truth that God has said.

Another father's doing is all this."
"So our legitimate birth You dismiss?!

Our only father's God!" "Were He, you'd love Me,
Since I was sent by Him who dwells above Me.

For I came not of My will, but was sent.
Why is My meaning not more evident?

You do not hear My words, nor is it truth you seek,
Because the father of all lies taught you to speak.

The devil is your father and you do his will,
Who's always sought the body and the soul to kill.

The devil only to his nature's true
When all words are deceitful through and through.

Because your father has no truth at all,
You think My words are folly, lies, and gall.

Could one of you convict Me of a single sin?
Then why are not My words what you put your faith in?

Who comes from God will listen to His word,
Ergo all I have said you have not heard."

179 "Before Abraham was, I AM"
Jn. 8:48-59

They asked, "Are you not governed by a demon?
Are not you from the Samaritan region?"

So He told them, "Untrue is every word and claim.
I give My Father honor while you'd give Me shame.

I don't Myself; another seeks My glory,
And of it He will be both judge and jury.

In truth, who keeps My word will never die."
"Now Your possession You cannot deny.

For Abraham died, God's prophets as well,
While You claim righteous men forever dwell.

Are You greater than Abraham, who died?
What is Your claim and how much is Your pride?"

"If I sought My own glory, it would hold no worth,
But it's conferred by Him, the Lord of all the earth,

The One you call your God, but Him you do not know.
If I denied I knew Him, I'd belong below

With you and him, the first and greatest liar,
Who lives forever in eternal fire.

For Abraham rejoiced to think My day he'd see,
And he, your father, saw it with such joie de vie."

The Jews said, "You are not fifty years old,
And you've seen Abraham?!" So they were told,

"In truth I tell you, before Abraham,
Before he even was conceived, I AM."

At this, the people picked up stones to heave,
So Jesus hid Himself that He might leave.

180 Jesus Heals the Man Born Blind
Jn. 9:1-41

Now, walking by, Christ met a man born blind.
Disciples asked, "Why was this cross assigned?

Did this man or his parents sin against the Lord?"
"Could babies sin before they cut the mother's cord?!?

What God gives punishment for what is not one's fault?
This man was blind so people might the Lord exalt

On seeing what great work was done for him.
For I am the world's light and can't go dim.

Until My life is like the setting sun, [157]
We have been given work that must be done.

The night when work cannot be done shall yet be faced."
Then Jesus spat upon the ground and made a paste,

Which He employed by rubbing on the blind man's eyes.
He said, "Go wash at Siloam for your sun to rise."[157]

(The name Siloam means "One who has been sent.")
Just then his disability was spent.

Now those who saw this blind beggar before
Debated who it was. Some people swore,

"It is not he, lest I've been taken for a fool."
"It sure is him, for frauds don't fall into the pool."[158]

The man himself said, "Truly, it is I."
"But you have never had a working eye.

How is it they were opened? Please explain."
"I do not understand, though it seemed plain.

The man who they call Jesus made a paste,
Then rubbed my eyes and said to go with haste

And wash them at Siloam, and when I did,
The world no longer from my eyes was hid."

They asked, "Where is He?" He said, "I don't know.
I still lacked sight when He got up to go."

The Jews then brought him to the Pharisees,
Who thought this Sabbath work would God displease.

They asked the man how he had gained his vision,
And when he told they made a harsh decision.

"One who keeps not the Sabbath can't be from the Lord."
Some said, "If not, then how has he a blind man cured?"

They were divided, so they asked the man
Just what he thought. "He said it was God's plan

That I be blind so others' faith will grow.
He truly is a prophet, this I know."

The Jews would not believe he was born blind
Until they could the beggar's parents find.

"We know your son was born blind. Is this he?
If so, how is it that he now can see?"

[250]

"That he's our son and was born blind we're sure,
But know not who or how the blind can cure.

Ask him. He's old enough to testify."
(They said this not to affirm nor deny,

Since they feared Jews, who first would reprimand,
And had, by now, from the synagogues banned

All who acknowledged Jesus as the Christ,
A bond that's not without pain sacrificed.)[159]

They called the man again and said, "Praise God!
We know we've seen through this sinner's façade."

"Whether He's sinned or not I have no knowledge,
But that He gave me sight I must acknowledge."

They asked, "What did He do? How was it done?"
"I have not lied, not since it's all begun.

I told what happened, in truth and complete.
Would you believe should I myself repeat?

Do you seek to His followers become?"
"Of course not, we do not know where He's from.

You follow Him, while we just Moses follow,
But this man's words we find too hard to swallow.

God spoke to Moses, giving him the Law,
Which this man broke." "But His good works you saw!

You do not know His source, but know His deeds.
Does God do works because a sinner pleads?

He surely is a righteous man who does God's will.
How many have cured men born blind? I know of nil.

Without the Lord, He couldn't do a thing."
"Do you think wisdom to us you can bring??!

You've been ridden with sin since you were born."
They threw him out and treated him with scorn.

Christ heard of this and sought the man out, lest he grieve,
"Have you faith in the Son of Man? Do you believe?"

"Just point Him out and I'll believe in Him."
"I am the Son, the light who will not dim."

The man said, "I believe," and offered praise.
"I came for men's judgment for endless days,

To give sight to the blind, with such precision,
And take the sight from those who trust their vision."

Some Pharisees heard this. "So we are blind, you say?"
"If only you were blind, your soul would be okay.

As long as you still your good sight maintain,
The guilt of it on your soul will remain."

181 "I am the Good Shepherd"
Jn. 10:1-18

"Who enters the sheepfold, not through the gate,
Is but a thief who comes to confiscate.

Who enters through the gate shepherds the flock.
And when the gatekeeper undoes the lock,

The sheep will hear his call and, one by one,
They'll go where he goes, run where he will run.

They follow him because they know his voice:
To follow strangers never is their choice.

If strangers came, the sheep would run away,
Not knowing either voice or what they say."

He told this parable to all those men,
But as they got it not, He spoke again,

"In truth, I tell you, I'm the sheepfold's gate.
Who came before Me came to confiscate,

But My good sheep remained, refused to follow
The voices they knew not, words that were hollow.

Who enters through this gate will be protected,
Led out to pasture, but never neglected.

The thief comes just to steal, kill, and destroy,
But I, that they have life, and full of joy.

I'm the good shepherd, who lays down His life.
While others might do so for son or wife,

I shall lay down My life, all for my little sheep.
A hired man, who works for pay, whose pay is cheap,

Will see a wolf and quickly run away,
For his concern's no greater than his pay.

Then when a wolf attacks, the sheep will flee.
I know My own sheep and My own know Me,

Just as I and the Father know each other.
I give My life for this fold and another.

For I must lead sheep from a different fold.
They, too, will hear My voice and do as told.

Then only one flock of sheep shall there be.
For doing this, the Father does love Me,

For laying down My life to take it up again.
The power to take life from Me rests not in men.

None take My life from Me; I lay it down,
Like when a king freely gives up his crown.

As freely chosen as My life I lose
Can I come back to life whene'er I choose,

Because My Father gave Me this command."

182 Division among the Jews again
Jn. 10:19-21

This split them more and each one took a stand:

"These are the ravings of a man possessed.
Why would you any words of His ingest?"

 "But were possessed His body and His mind,
How could He make see eyes that once were blind?"

Chapter X
The Ministry in Judea

183 On Divorce and Celibacy[160]
Mt. 19:3-12, Mk. 10:2-12

Now Pharisees came up to Christ to test,
"If one's divorced, has he the Law transgressed?"

"From Moses, what command did you receive?"
"Men can divorce their wives and have them leave."

"'Twas tolerated for the hardness of your heart.
Yet things were not in this perverse state from the start.

Have you not read that male and female they were made?
Hence men leave parents and the home at which they've stayed.

They are one flesh, and nearly share a heart.
What God has joined no man should tear apart.[161]

All who divorce their wives, and then remarry
The sin of an adulterer will carry."

The twelve replied, "Then marriage is not well-advised."
"Not all can live thus and should not be criticized.

Some eunuchs are from birth and some are made this way.
Some do this to themselves, since bodies will decay,

Forsaking pleasure for eternal life.
Who has this gift should live without a wife."[162]

184 Jesus Blesses the Children
Mt. 19:13-15, Mk. 10:13-16, Lk. 18:15-17

Then children, some only a few months old,
Were brought for Him to bless, pray for, and hold.

His followers rebuked these people, yet
This made Jesus indignant and upset,

 "When children seek Me, they shan't be rejected.
Such as these shall for heaven be selected.

You'll either enter heaven like a child
Or elsewhere go, where no one ever smiled."

He took the children, showed them agape,
Laid hands upon them, and then went away.

185 The Rich Young Man
Mt. 19:16-22, Mk. 10:17-22, Lk. 18:18-23

A man ran up to Him, knelt down as if to plead,
"Good teacher, life eternal is gained by what deed?"

"Why do you call Me this? For only God is good.
The Ten Commandments limit men to what they should:

You shall not kill. You shan't commit adultery.
You shall not steal, nor shall you commit perjury.

Do not defraud. Obey father and mother,
And, as you love yourself, love one another.'"

"All these have I observed since I was young." [163]
Christ said, "If truth is coming from your tongue,

One virtue to be perfect you still lack.
Go home, where your possessions you must pack

To sell them all and give it to the poor.
Then shall you have treasure for evermore.

And once you've left it all, come, follow Me."
The man left sad, so burdened down was he.

186 On the Danger of Riches and the Rewards of Discipleship
Mt. 19:23-30, Mk. 10:23-31, Lk. 18:24-30

Christ then told His disciples, "Not with ease
Can rich men bypass Mephistopheles.[164]

For riches are such a dark source of evil
That easier through the eye of a needle

Could pass a camel than a rich man could
Get into heaven, with his livelihood."

They questioned this, it gave them such surprise,
"Who's saved, if wealth can kill a soul like lies?"

"What is not possible with men their God can do." [165]
Said Peter, "We left everything to follow You."

"In truth, when I shall sit upon My throne,
On Judgment Day, when deeds and hearts are known,

You twelve shall judge the tribes of Israel,
Bringing to heaven, casting down to hell.

For anyone who gave up family
Or wealth or lands, for My Gospel and Me,

Will gain a hundredfold and paradise.
Thus shall God give to those who sacrifice.

The one who is in earthly riches first
Will find his place for all times is the worst."

187 The Parable of the Laborers in the Vineyard
Mt. 20:1-16

"God's kingdom's like a man who owns some land,
And went to get many a helping hand

To work all day, and so it was agreed
He'd pay one denarius for the deed.

This man went out again, asking at nine,
'Who wants to pick my grapes to make great wine?

I promise that a fair wage I will pay.'
In his field they spent the rest of the day.

He went again to find more, then, at noon.
'To wages win, get to my vineyard soon.'

He went once more at three and then at five,
For more workers would make his business thrive.

He asked, 'Why have, all day, you idle been?'
'If one would hire, work we would begin.'

He said, 'You go into my vineyard, too.'
Then, to his bailiff, 'First please pay the few

Who came last, likewise till the first you pay.'
They got a denarius for the day.

When those who came first saw his generosity,
They hopeful grew, with greedy curiosity.

But when they, too, were given the same wage,
They grumbled at him and were filled with rage,

'Some worked one hour and received the same!
We worked all day under the sun's hot flame!'

'You can't complain, for nothing did you lose.
Can I not with my own do what I choose?

Leave with your wage, I paid as we agreed.
My gift should not cause jealousy and greed.'

The first shall be last, the last shall be first.
In heaven, these things will all be reversed."

188 Jesus at the Feast of Dedication in Jerusalem
Jn. 10:22-39

At winter, at the feast of Dedication,
Christ was in Temple for the celebration

And, walking past Solomon's Portico,
Jews asked, "How much more till You let us know?

If You're the Christ, just say so that we might perceive."
"I have already, and you still do not believe.

The works that I do in My Father's name
Attest to Me, but you remain the same.

You don't believe because you're not My sheep:
My sheep belong to Me and My words keep.

I know them and they follow to a tee,
And I give to them life eternally.

They never shall be lost, but know the land
And they shall not be stolen from My hand.

He gave Me this and greater is than anyone.
None can steal from the Father; He and I are one."

The Jews picked rocks up for their Christ to stone.
He asked, "With all the good works I have shown,

Why do you all want to throw stones at Me?"
"It's not for works, but for Your blasphemy.

For You are man and men come from the sod,
While You have made a claim that You are God."

"'I said you're gods,'[166] is written in your Law.
Those who relay His Word without a flaw

Are thus referred, and Scripture can't be set aside.
Yet whom the Father sent to this world you deride,

'You have blasphemed to say You are God's Son!'
Now if My Father's work I had not done,

There would not be a need that you believe Me.
Yet if I do, though you do not receive Me,

Had you faith in My works, then you would see
I'm in the Father just as He's in Me."

They sought then to arrest Jesus again,
But He eluded all the plotting men.

189 Jesus Withdraws across the Jordan
Jn. 10:40-42

Christ went back to the Jordan's other side,
Where John baptized, to briefly there reside.

Crowds came, believing in Him, "No signs did John do,
But all he said about this man was clearly true."

190 The Raising of Lazarus
Jn. 11:1-44

A man named Lazarus of Bethany
Was friends with Christ, as was his family.

The girls sent word, to urgency instill,
"Our brother whom You love is gravely ill!"

To people's shock, when Jesus heard this news,
He said, "This will not make our brother lose

His life. Contrarily, the reason for it
Is to exalt God so none can ignore it."

Although He loved them, Jesus did not move,
Nor did the state of Lazarus improve,

For two whole days. Then Jesus showed concern,
"We all shall now to Judea return."

"But Rabbi, it's not long since people there
Tried stoning You. You think Your life they'll spare?"

Christ said, "Is not the day twelve hours long?
Those who go by its light will not go wrong,

But he will stumble who walks 'round at night,
Not knowing where he's going without light.

For Lazarus is sleeping. I must wake him."
His followers heard this, but were mistaken:

"If he is just asleep, then he'll be fine."
"I mean that his illness is not benign.

Our Lazarus has passed away, and glad am I
We were not there, so this would your faith magnify.

[265]

His death will only briefly make them grim."
Then Thomas said, "Let's go to die with him."

When they arrived they found the tears were steady,
For he was in the tomb four days already.

As they were two miles from the holy city,
A multitude of Jews came giving pity.[167]

When these sisters saw Jesus had arrived,
Martha came to him, "He would have survived!!

If you were here, I know he'd not have died!
And, still, whate'er you ask God will provide."

So He assured her, "He will rise again."
"I know he shall, as will all righteous men

At the resurrection on the last day."
"I'm the resurrection, in truth I say.

Whoe'er believes, although they die, will live.
They will not really die, for I shall give

Eternal life to them. Do you believe?"
"I know you came to earth to give reprieve,

The Christ who walks among us to save Israel."
On hearing this, she went for her sister to tell,

"The master's here and wants to talk to you."
And she got up so fast she nearly flew.

He still was far away, where he and Martha met,
But, still, the Jews, who knew that she was so upset,

Went with her, thinking she would go to weep
At the tomb where Lazarus lay asleep.

The second Mary did her master meet
She quickly threw herself down at His feet,

"If You were here, I know he'd not have died!"
Moved by her tears, and the crowd, He replied,

"Where have you put him?" They said, "Come and see."
At this, the eyes of Christ welled heavily.

The Jews said, "His love for the man none could deny,"
But others asked, "If He could heal a blind man's eye,

Then why could He not have his death prevented?"
Christ, seeing how the girls were so tormented,

Went to the tomb and had them move the stone,
But Martha protested, "His flesh and bone

Are four days rotting and will surely smell."
Yet Jesus said to her, "Did I not tell

That for your faith God's glory you would see?"
Then Jesus turned from this, looked upwardly,

"I thank You, Father, for hearing My prayer.
You always hear, but I ask for their share,

That those around Me might see and believe,
That their inheritance they may receive."

He cried out loudly, "Lazarus, come out!"
And, instantly, the Christ removed all doubt,

For out walked Lazarus, though four days dead.
"He is the resurrection!" people said.

Christ told those people, overcome with shock,
"Unbind the man who's now free from the rock."

191 The Chief Priests and Pharisees Plot against Jesus
Jn. 11:45-57

Now, many Jews, who came for to console
Came to believe that Christ could save their soul

And give them life, while others went to tell
The Pharisees the strange things that befell.

The chief priests then met with the Pharisees,
"We must say, 'You cannot do as You please,'

Or else take action. Were His words to spread,
Then Rome would come and leave our land for dead."

Then Caiaphas, who was chief priest that year,
Said, "Don't you see that He must disappear?

It benefits you that one man should die
Rather than all of Israel should fry."

He spoke, not on his own, but as high priest,
And prophesied why Christ would be deceased,

To save the whole nation of Israel
And gather God's lost kids wheree'er they dwell.

From then they were determined Christ must die
And, knowing this, He did not just stand by

Because when He would die was preordained.
He went to Ephraim and there He remained

[268]

With His disciples, for He did not choose
To any longer walk amongst the Jews.[168]

Now, as the Passover was drawing near,
Some pilgrims wondered, "Will Jesus come here?"

The chief priests and the Pharisees had sent out word
That Jews must tell Christ's whereabouts, whate'er they'd heard.

192 The Third Prediction of the Passion
Mt. 20:17-19, Mk. 10:32-34, Lk. 18:31-34

On the road leading to Jerusalem,
They walked, with Jesus well ahead of them.

Those with Him feared the wrath for His renown,
Though no harsh threat nor wind could slow Him down.

Christ told the twelve, "We're heading to the city
Where priests and scribes will treat Me without pity,

Condemning Me to die at Gentile hands,
Who gladly heed unto all cruel demands.

I'll be arrested and severely whipped,
My kingship made fun of and My clothes stripped,

My body crucified, yet this demise
Will not last for, on the third day, I'll rise."

These things were still not by them comprehended,
But that they would remember Christ intended.

193 Precedence among the Disciples
Mt. 20:20-28, Mk. 10:35-45

The mother of the sons of Zebedee
Begged Christ, "Would you grant anything for me?"

"What is it you would have Me do for you?"
"It's nothing for myself, but my sons two.

As each of them is kneeling at my side,
When You're enthroned, that they each sit beside."

"What you are asking is not what you think.
Can you drink from the cup from which I drink?"

Then James and John asserted, "We are able."
"Though we may share a loaf and cup at table,

It is not I by whom the crown is shared,
But for My Father, who My thrown prepared."

On hearing this, the other ten were fuming,
And with their pride and jealousy consuming,

They argued who was greatest in their lot.
"You know how Gentiles make known all they've got,

How they lord over men with their authority.
You must, like Me, not seek superiority.

The first among you must act as a slave;
The eldest must as if he's young behave.

[271]

Although important men may sit at table,
The truly great serve others, as they're able.

To serve, not to be served, the Son is driven,
To give His life for man, as ransom's given.

194 The Healing of the Blind Man, Bartimaeus
Mt. 20:29-34, Mk. 10:46-52, Lk. 18:35-43

Now, as they were approaching Jericho,
A massive multitude with Christ did go.

Now, sitting by the roadside, Bartimaeus,
A beggar blind and the son of Timaeus,

On hearing that a crowd gathered, asked why.
"Jesus of Nazareth is passing by."

"Have mercy on me, Jesus, David's Son!"
Though he was then rebuked by everyone,

This only made him scream out all the more,
"Have mercy on me!" till his throat was sore.

So Christ commanded he be brought to Him.
They said, "He's called for you, look not so grim!"

He came to Christ, who asked, "What can I grant you?"
"Please give me sight, for this grand world I can't view."

"Receive your sight at once; your faith has made you see."
He followed Christ, praising the Lord with joi de vie.

195 Zacchaeus
Lk. 19:1-10

At this time, as Christ passed through Jericho,
A man whose rank was high, but stature low,

A rich man named Zacchaeus, struggled to see Christ.
Yet, for the crowds, no efforts that he made sufficed.

He ran ahead and climbed a sycamore
So he could see Christ, since He failed before.

Christ passed and said, "You elsewhere should recline.
Tonight, Zacchaeus, with you we shall dine."

He hurried and though he was filled with joy,
What honored him did other men annoy:

"That's no way to a faithless sinner treat!"
"Why would He with a tax collector eat?!"

"I never would with such a man be found!"
Zacchaeus heard this and he stood his ground,

"Half of my property I shall give to the poor.
And anyone I've cheated I'll pay back times four."

"I came to save while other men would damn,
For you, too, are a son of Abraham.

The Son of Man has come, at any cost,
To seek out and bring back those who are lost."

196 The Anointing at Bethany
Mt. 26:6-13, Mk. 14:3-9, Jn. 12:1-8

When Passover was still six days away,
Jesus with Lazarus' kin did stay.

They gave a dinner at which Martha served
And Mary, in thanksgiving unreserved,

Poured on His feet an ointment of pure nard.
And, as she held Him in such high regard,

She wiped them with her hair, a fitting tribute.
Yet Judas asked, "Why did she not contribute

Its three hundred denarii cost to those in need?"
(He said this not from charity, but out of greed.

For he controlled their group's communal cash,
And stole from it, gaining a growing stash.)

So Jesus said, "Why should you bother her?
It's good before My body they inter

It be anointed. You will always have the poor,
While fairly soon I won't be with you anymore.

Around the world, where they preach My good news,
They will recall how she did her gifts use."

197 The Plot against Lazarus
Jn. 12:9-11

At this time, many Jews[169] followed Him there,
Not just for Christ, but since they were aware

That Lazarus had been raised from the dead.
So some were coming to see him instead.

The Chief priests then decided both of them should die,
For he was proof and soon all men would testify.

For his accounts did men the chief priests leave
And in the words of Jesus Christ believe.

Chapter XI
The Final Ministry in Jerusalem

198 The Triumphal Entry: Jesus is Praised with Palm
Mt. 21:1-9, Mk. 11:1-10, Lk. 19:28-40, Jn. 12:12-19

Then, as they all approached Jerusalem,
From Jericho, where they were coming from,

Near Bethpage, Bethany, or thereabout,
At the Mount of Olives, Christ sent two out,

"Go to the village that lies opposite.
You'll find a donkey on which I must sit,

Once you arrive, there with its foal beside,
And I need that these two beasts be untied.

Should someone think that something is amiss,
And question you, 'Why are you doing this?',

Just say, 'The Lord has need of them and will
Return them once His purpose they fulfill.'"

And this fulfilled the words the prophet said,
"Tell Zion's daughter, 'Hark! Behold ahead,

Where, humbly, on a donkey, rides your king
And on a colt, the donkey's dear offspring.'"

So these two went and did just as directed,
And they found all things as they had expected.

They, on their own then, for Jesus' benefit,
Lay their garments on ass and colt, where He would sit.

When He rode them, a crowd gathered around
And threw their clothes and branches on the ground.

They praised the Lord for works their Christ had done,
Crying, "Hosanna unto David's Son![170]

Blessed is He who comes in our Lord's name!
Peace be above and infinite acclaim!

Blest, too, be David's kingdom, now restored!
Hosanna in the highest! Praise the Lord!"

Now many in the crowd were present when
He told a corpse to rise and walk again,

And Lazarus, though four days dead, arose.
They thought he could do naught but decompose. [171]

So those who saw this miracle this good news spread
And crowds came seeking Him who raised men from the dead.

Some Pharisees said, "Rabbi, stop this praise extreme!"
Christ said, "If they were mute, the very stones would scream."

They said amongst themselves, the only ones there grim,
"We can't do anything; the world's gone after Him."

199 Jesus Weeps over Jerusalem
Lk. 19:41-44

Christ saw Jerusalem and His tears would not cease,
"If even now you knew the things that make for peace![172]

But now these things are hidden from your eyes.
Against you shall great armies mobilize.

These men will surround you with forts built around you.
You'll hide in your walls, but their weapons will pound through.

Your children won't be safe in walls or womb.
They shall dash heads and fire will consume.

And not one stone shall stay in its location,
For knowing not when was your visitation."

200 The Cursing of the Fig Tree[173]
Mt. 21:18-19, Mk. 11:12-14

The next day, as Christ went from Bethany,
He hungered as He spotted a fig tree,

And, coming closer, saw the tree was bare.
"You always shall be fruitless, I declare,"

Christ cursed the fig tree and He passed it by
And towards Jerusalem He turned His eye.

201 Jesus Overturns the Tables of the Money Changers[174]
Mt. 21:10-17, Mk. 11:15-17, Lk. 19:45-46, Jn. 2:14-22

As He was passing through, the city stirred,
"This is the prophet and He speaks God's word,

Called Jesus, Christ, from Nazareth in Galilee."
Christ went into the Temple, furious to see

The men by whom the oxen, sheep and doves were sold
And those who gave men Jewish coins for Roman gold.

He drove them out, using a whip of cord
And all their coins, then, on the floor He poured.

He overturned the tables, tossed seats in the air,
"It's written, 'My house must be called a house of prayer,'[175]

Yet you are making it a robber's den!"[176]
This greatly angered all the leading men,

For blind and lame approached Him to be healed,
And children's excitement was not concealed.

"Hosanna to the Son of David!" was their song.
The scribes and chief priests saw this, "Tell them how they're wrong."

So Jesus said to them, "Have you not read,
'Out of the mouths of little babes is said

The greatest praise that ever has been spoken.'?"[177]
"For all these things You've thrown about and broken,

For all the praise You've willingly received,
What sign have You that You should be believed?"

"Destroy this Temple and in just three days,
What you have made mere rubble I will raise."

"You can rebuild what's forty-six years taken? [178]
If you think so, you grossly are mistaken."

Yet it was not the Temple they were in He meant,
But to predict His body's fate was His intent.

202 The Chief Priests and Scribes Conspire against Jesus
Mk. 11:18-19, Lk. 19:47-48

The chief priests and the scribes sought His destruction,
But people closely followed His instruction.

So strongly did they feel His words were true
That priests and scribes found nothing they could do.

203 The Withered Fig Tree
Mt. 21:20-22, Mk. 11:20-26

That morning, they passed by the tree that gave no fruit
And marveled that it had been withered to the root,

"Behold! The tree has withered, all by Your command!"
"With faith in God, you'll one day do works far more grand.

You'll tell a mountain, 'Go into the sea,'
And if you do not doubt it, it will be.

For what you ask in prayer you will receive:
The Lord will hear His children who believe.

When praying, you must pardon all who wrong you,
Or have no mercy from Him you belong to."

204 The Question about Authority
Mt. 21:23-27, Mk. 11:27-33, Lk. 20:1-8

As Christ was teaching in the Temple, He was met
By chief priests, scribes, and elders, who were most upset,

 "By what authority do You these actions do?
Or who then is it who gave this command to You?"

 "I'll answer yours if you will answer Mine.
Was John's Baptism earthly or divine?

Came it from heaven or was it from men?"
They argued, "If we say from heaven, then

They'll ask us 'Where were you when John sought to baptize?
Why are your legs in disagreement with your eyes?'"

 "But if we say his words were just from earth,
They'll question both our judgment and our worth."

So they said, "We do not know, we concede."
"Then without telling you will I proceed."

205 The Parable of the Two Sons
Mt. 21:28-32

"What would you think? A man once two sons had,
Who told them what to do and what's forbade.

The first boy was out to the vineyard sent.
He fist said 'No,' but thought again and went.

He also asked the second, who replied,
'By anything you say will I abide.'

Although he said this, what he did was nil.
I ask you which one did his father's will?"

"The first," they said, and no one did dispute.
"The tax collector and the prostitute

Shall beat you to the kingdom of the Lord.
When John repentance from their sins implored,

They learned from him the path to righteousness,
And, seeing this, his words you still dismiss.

Your claims to righteousness are quite absurd,
For, like the second son, they're just a word."

206 The Parable of the Wicked Husbandmen
Mt. 21:33-46, Mk. 12:1-12, Lk. 20:9-19

"Another parable I have to tell.
A vineyard-owner left to elsewhere dwell

And leased it to some tenants for the year.
Months later, when the vintage time drew near,

Some servants came the produce to collect.
One servant they left beaten, badly wrecked.

Then others were assaulted, even slain.
The owner thought, 'My son they'll not disdain.

If anyone, my son they will respect.'
And so the son was sent out to collect.

On seeing him, they said to one another,
'Let's kill the son, the heir who has no brother,

For then the owner's vineyard we could claim.'
And, as they killed before, they did the same.

They cast him from the vineyard, where they slew.
When he returns, what will the owner do?"

"He'll kill those wretches in a vicious way,
And lend his land to tenants who will pay."

Christ asked those listening, "Have you not Scripture read?
The stone rejected has become the corner's head.

This vindication surely is God's doing.
How blest is every eye that this is viewing!

For those who fall upon that stone will break like glass,
While any underneath, will flattened be like grass."

At this, the priests and scribes sought to arrest,
But feared how might the multitude protest.

They knew the story was against them told,
But folks know when a prophet they behold.

207 The Parable of the Great Supper
Mt. 22:1-14, Lk. 14:15-24

On hearing this, one of those gathered round
Said to the Christ, "How blest are all those found

Invited to the feasts the Lord will give."
"Not all invited will forever live.

A king once gave a feast when his son married.
Reminders had been by the servants carried:

'Come and rejoice with us! All is prepared!
A kingly feast is waiting to be shared!'

They gave excuses why they'd not attend:
'I've bought ten oxen which I have to tend.'

'I have just married.' 'I have just bought land.
Please send apologies, he'll understand.'

And some unto the slaves were not so nice
And showed their hearts were filled with naught but vice.

Some slaves were seized and beaten, even killed.
The king heard and was with such anger filled

He sent out soldiers to destroy those men
And burn their homes. He sent his slaves again,

'Invite the poor, the crippled, lame, and blind.'
And after this, the king at last reclined

Only to hear, 'My lord, we've empty seats.'
So he replied, 'Since you have searched the streets,

Look outside of the town. Search far and wide
To share the joy of my son and his bride.

Those who stayed home can starve for all I care!'
Then, at his feast, no single seat was bare,

That is, until the king saw that one guest
Was at his party improperly dressed.

He asked, 'Who let you in sans wedding garment?'[179]
With no response, he said, 'Throw out this varmint!

Unto this man, his hands and feet you'll bind.
Toss him where tears burst forth and teeth do grind,

Where darkness is complete and does not end.'
All are invited, but far less attend."

208 The Question about Paying Tribute to Caesar
Mt. 22:15-22, Mk. 12:13-17, Lk. 20:20-26

The Pharisees attempted trapping Him again,
So they approached Him with a few of Herod's men,

All praising Christ with words most insincere,
"We know Your words are true and hold them dear.

You have no bias, nor seek human praise,
And what You teach men truly are God's ways.

Does paying Caesar taxes break the Law?"
He knew their malice, through their hearts He saw,

 "Why put Me to the test, you hypocrite?
Show Me a coin,[180] that I may look on it."

Then, seeing it, He asked, "Whose image does it bear?"
And they responded to Him, "Caesar's face is there."

 "So render unto Caesar what's his own,
But give to God all that is His alone."

They heard His teaching and could not deny it,
So they left Christ in awe, in shame, and quiet.

209 The Question about the Resurrection
Mt. 22:23-33, Mk. 12:18-27, Lk. 20:27-40

Some Sadducees thought they could give correction
(And they believed there is no resurrection),

And so they tested Christ with, "Moses said
A woman childless, with husband dead,

Should by the brother of her spouse be married.
There was a woman who no children carried.

This law was followed when her husband died,
But still no children did the Lord provide.

The same occurred with her and brothers seven.
Now whose wife is she when she gets to heaven?"

 "You are mistaken and your thoughts absurd.
You neither know God's power nor His Word.

For unlike this world, in the afterlife,
The risen neither have husband nor wife.

They are like angels, sharing their perfection,
These sons of God and of the resurrection.

And, speaking of the resurrection of the dead,
Have you not read the words that God to Moses said,

 'I am your God, the God of Abraham,
Of Isaac and Jacob. I Am Who Am.'

He's not God of the dead, but of the living."
The crowds loved all the answers He was giving.

210 The Great Commandment
Mt. 22:34-40, Mk. 12:28-34

Then, seeing how He silenced Sadducees,
A lawyer came, one of the Pharisees,

To ask, "Of all commandments, which one is the first?"
Christ said, "The one which leaves men most blest or accursed

Is 'God is one, and should be loved in whole,
With all your heart and mind and strength and soul.'

Then 'As you love yourself, love one another,
Both neighbor, kin, friend, foe, and any other.

On these the prophets as well as all laws depend."
The scribe said, "Well do You the Scriptures comprehend.

That God is one and there's no other You are right.
To love God with your mind, your soul, your heart and might

And love your neighbor as yourself suffices
More than all offerings and sacrifices."

Christ said, "You're not far from the kingdom of the Lord."
From then to challenge Jesus no one could afford.

211 The Question about David's Son
Mt. 22:41-46, Mk. 12:35-37a, Lk. 20:41-44

He taught, "How can they say the Christ is David's son?
For David said, when speaking of the Promised One,

'The Lord said to my Lord, "Come, sit ay My right hand,
Until I make your enemies kneel where you stand."'

So how's the Christ his son if he's called 'Lord'?"
From then, to challenge Christ none could afford.[181]

212 Woe to the Scribes and Pharisees
Mt. 23:1-36, Mk. 12:37b-40, Lk. 20:45-47

To His disciples and the crowds, Christ said,
"By scribes and Pharisees have you been lead

And this is fine. You must do as they say,
But from their words their deeds are far away.

From Moses do they have the right to teach,
But rarely do they practice what they preach.

They bind up heavy burdens, hard to bear,
And lay them on men's shoulders without care,

And for it they would not a finger lift.
They only to gain honor give a gift.

They make their headbands broad and tassels long[182]
And seek places of honor to belong,

The highest places when at synagogue or feast,
And being known as 'rabbi', so their pride's increased.

By this name you should not each other call:
You have one teacher, you are brothers all.

Call no man 'father': you are each God's son.
And call none 'master': you are owned by one.

No titles that show honor should you seek:
A man is only great when he is meek.

The greatest of you, he shall serve the rest.
By men of high rank God is not impressed.

He who exalts himself will be brought down,
Whereas the humble man will gain renown.

Woe to you hypocrites, both scribes and Pharisees,
Who turn God's children into heaven's enemies!

You won't see heaven, so great is your sin
And you stop others from entering in.

Woe to you hypocrites, you scribes and Pharisees!
To make a proselyte, you travel many seas.

Your effort's wasted, though you travel far.
You make them twice the demon that you are.

Woe to the scribe and Pharisee, the hypocrite!
You swallow widow's houses for your benefit,

And for a pretense will you make long prayer,
So you'll receive the worst damnation there.

Woe to you, guides who have not sight, who say,
'If one swears on the Temple, then he may

His promise break, but who swears on its gold
Must do it all, exactly as he told.'

You sightless fools! Which is more sacred of the twain?
That gold or Yahweh's place, which makes it not mundane?

You say swears by the altar do not mean a thing,
Unlike swears by the altar's gift that people bring.

You men most blind! Which one is greater of the two?
The gift or what sets gifts apart, I ask of you?

To swear by one's to swear by all that's on it.
For either, do not falsely swear upon it.

To swear by heaven swears upon the throne
And on the one who does the kingdom own.

Woe to you, for you tithe mint, dill, and cumin,
Neglecting love of God and fellow human.

You heed the least and break the greater one:
The laws of mercy must the first be done.

You blind guides, who men never ought to follow!
You strain a gnat out but a camel swallow!

Woe to you, hypocrite, both scribe and Pharisee!
The outside of the cup and dish, what people see,

Is cleaned, but inside, filled to its capacity,
With wickedness, extortion, and rapacity!

Did not who made the outside make what lies within?
Give alms till cups are bare and you'll be cleansed of sin!

Woe to you, scribe and Pharisee, both hypocrite!
For, as a whitewashed tomb, you outwardly look fit,

But inside they are full of dead man's bones.
You're equally unclean behind your stones!

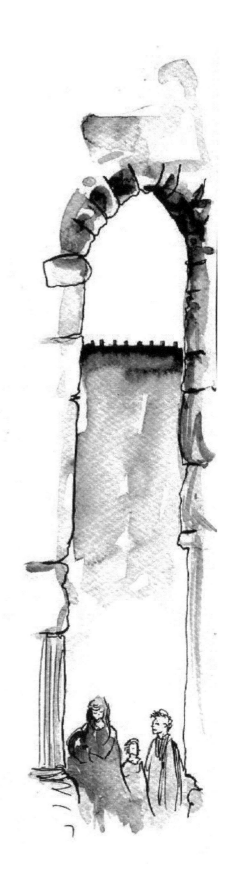

[297

So much you strive that righteous you appear.
You're hypocritical and insincere!

Great woe to you, adorning tombs of righteous men
And prophets, while you claim, 'If we had lived back then,

Back in our fathers' time, when prophets' blood was shed,
It would not be by our hands that the prophets bled.

You testify that you are truly sons
Of those who killed the Lord's anointed ones.

So claim what from your fathers you inherit.
You brood of vipers, hell is all you merit!

Therefore, I send you prophets, scribes, wise men
You'll kill, scourge, or throw in a lion's den.

Some you will scourge in synagogues to knock them down,
While others you will persecute from town to town.

All righteous blood e'er shed will then your own hands stain,
From Abel, who was innocent, but killed by Cain,

And all those through the blood of Zechariah,
The fearless, righteous son of Barachiah,

Who perished by the altar, at his station.[183]
All this will come upon this generation."

213 Jesus' Lament over Jerusalem
Mt. 23:37-39, Lk. 13:34-35

O, My Jerusalem, the prophets you have killed,
The blood of those sent by the Lord you've always spilled.

I would, like mother hens, your children gather,
Under her wings, yet other things you'd rather.

Forsaken and deserted are your house,
Devoid of children, parents, friends, or spouse.

You'll not see Me again till these words are outpoured,
'Blessed is he who comes in the name of the Lord.'"[184]

214 The Generosity of the Poor Widow
Mk. 12:41-44, Lk. 21:1-4

Christ sat down by the treasury and saw
Crowds giving coins, as called for by the Law.

The rich gave much, a poor widow a penny,
And Christ said, "She has given more than any,

For out of their abundance they are giving,
While she has given her entire living."

Chapter XII
The Eschatological Discourse[185]

215 Prediction of the Destruction of the Temple
Mt. 24:1-2, Mk. 13:1-2, Lk. 21:5-6

As Jesus left the Temple, one disciple said,
"Look at these buildings, how they tower overhead!"

"These stones will not last! What can will be burned
And not one stone will not be overturned!"

216 Signs before the End
Mt. 24:3-8, Mk. 13:3-8, Lk. 21:7-11

They asked Him, "Teacher, when and what signs will appear
To show that all these things You prophesied are near?"

Christ said, "Take heed that you're not led astray.
For men will come in My name and will say,

'I am the Christ!' and 'The time is at hand!'
They will mislead those who don't understand.

When you hear of wars and rumors thereof,
Do not think judgment comes yet from above.

For nation shall clash fiercely against nation,
While kingdoms fight, and throughout all creation,

Both pestilence and famine will abound,
While massive earthquakes shall shake up the ground.

Great signs and terrors will leave men's heads spinning,
And for the birth pangs this is the beginning."

217 Persecutions Foretold
Mt. 24:9-14, Mk. 13:9-13, Lk. 21:12-19

"For you shall be delivered up to die.
They'll seize you from your homes, to terrify,

And bring you to both jail and synagogue
To pummel, mock, to deprecate and flog.

To governors and kings you'll testify,
But do not worry how you will reply.

What you need say the Spirit will inspire,
Who comes in silence, comes through wind and fire.

So do not fear the trials you cannot predict.
The Spirit will give words they cannot contradict.

Then brothers will deliver up their brothers,
Fathers their children and children their mothers,

And many will be killed because of their own kin.
They'll harm you for My name, which you put your faith in.

He who holds true throughout all will be saved.
In places where they're morally depraved,

Such that they persecute who spreads My word,
Leave there, so that by others you are heard.

In truth, the Son of Man will come before
You've reached each Jewish town, from shore to shore.[186]

A student's not above the one who taught,
But likeness to the teacher is well sought.

If by 'Beelzebul' people your master call,
No better will upon those of My house befall.

Then many will betray their friends, apostatize,
And hate each other and false prophets will arise.

Most men's hearts will grow cold when there is strife,
But who endures will gain eternal life.

Throughout the world My message will extend.
All this will happen; then will come the end."

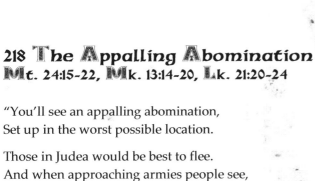

218 The Appalling Abomination
Mt. 24:15-22, Mk. 13:14-20, Lk. 21:20-24

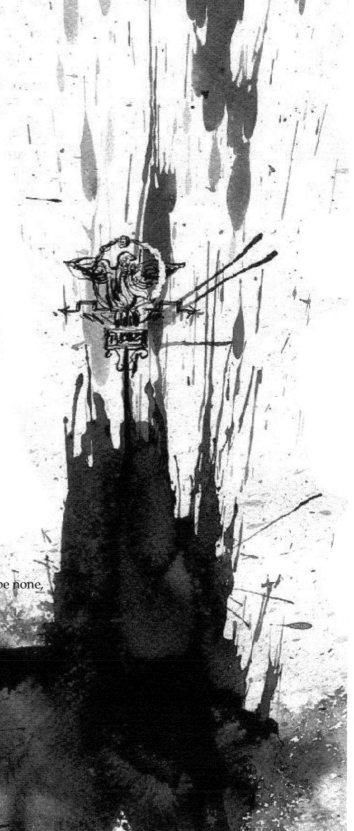

"You'll see an appalling abomination,
Set up in the worst possible location.

Those in Judea would be best to flee.
And when approaching armies people see,

Those on the rooftops must leave what's below behind.
Fieldworkers must not be by anything confined.

Let those inside the city flee at once,
And all outside avoid the battlefronts.

Such woe and heartache shall befall the city
That all who hear it shall be filled with pity.

Alas for those with child in those days
And mothers who young nursing babies raise!

In those days, there will be such tribulation,
Such as has never happened since creation,

And, after it, will never be again.
For many women, small children, and men

Will fall upon the sword, while people who survive
As captive slaves in all lands gentile will arrive,

The city laid waste and its people killed
Until the time of Gentiles is fulfilled.

Had not these days been shortened, those saved would be none,
But for the sake of the elect will this be done."

219 False Christ's and False Prophets
Mt. 24:23-28, Mk. 13:21-23, Lk. 17:23-24, 37b

"You'll long to see a day from after My return,
But eyes will not, as much as hearts may deeply burn.

If someone tells you, 'Look, there is the Christ!'
You must not be so easily enticed.

False Christ's and prophets will arise and show great signs
To mislead those for whom the Lord a place assigns.

As you have been warned, be aware of this.
Should you hear, 'He is in the wilderness,'

Do not go there. If they say, 'In the inner room,'
Concern for this should not a moment's thought consume.

Just as a flash of lightning shines across the sky,
The Son of Man's arrival shall meet every eye.

For where the body lies upon the ground
Above you'll see the vultures fly around."

Yet first the Son will meet grief and privation
And be rejected by this generation."

220 The Coming of the Son of Man
Mt. 24:29-31, Mk. 13:24-27, Lk. 21:25-28

"In those days, when has passed the tribulation,
The sun and moon will lack illumination,

While countless stars fall down out of the sky
And, everywhere, great pains will terrify.

The oceans and the seas and their turmoil
Will make men faint and, in their fear, recoil.

The powers of the heavens will be shaken
And all tribes will by grief be overtaken

When people see the coming of the Son of Man,
In majesty not seen since all the world began.

From clouds of heaven will He send His angels forth
To gather God's children from west, east, south and north."

221 The Parable of the Fig Tree
Mt. 24:32-36, Mk. 13:28-32, Lk. 21:29-33

"Now from the fig a lesson you should learn.
When it grows leaves, the summer soon will burn.

So, too, when you see all these things appear,
You know the coming of the Son is near.

Before passes away this generation
Each word will come true of this divination.

Though heavens and the earth will pass away,
The words I've taught to you will always stay.

The Father knows the hour, but no other one,
Not angels up in heaven or even the Son."

222 "Take Heed, Watch!"
Mk. 13:33-37, Lk. 21:34-36

"So take heed and keep watch, as you don't know
When your soul from the world of men will go.

It's like a man who on a journey is to roam.
Beforehand, he puts servants in charge of his home,

With each one having his responsibility
To handle to the best of his ability.

So do your task with detail and concern,
Not knowing when your master will return.

For He could come at evening or midnight,
The middle of the day, or dawn's first light.

If in debauchery a servant's found,
If drunk, hungover, passed out on the ground,

The master's coming will bring tribulation.
Make sure the master finds you've kept your station.

This day shall meet all those who are alive.
Pray always for the strength that you survive,

For much will men endure, as is God's plan,
Before they stand before the Son of Man."

Chapter XIII
The End Draws Near

223 The Parable of the Flood and Exhortation to Watchfulness
Mt. 24:37-44, Mk. 13:35, Lk. 17:26-36, 12:39-40

"Make sure to gird your loins and keep lamps burning,
And be like slaves whose masters are returning,

Who wait while he attends a wedding feast.
Once he arrives are his door's locks released.

Blest are those servants whom the master finds alert.
He'd have them seated and prepare for them dessert.

If in the second or the third watch of the night
He finds them thus, then greater will be their delight.

If householders knew when a thief would come,
They would not let themselves be stolen from.

[310]

Likewise, the Son will come most unexpectedly.
Stand ready, for the hour you cannot foresee.

This all will come to man as did the flood,
When men were drowned by rain, stuck in the mud.

For in those days, they ate, drank, and were married,
And cared for wealth, but not the guilt they carried.

For pleasure was enjoyed and wealth was hoarded
Up till the time that Noah's ark was boarded.

Then came the rains and swept them all away.
The Son's arrival will be in this way.

In Lot's time, farms and shops were well maintained
Until the fires from the heavens rained.

Recall how Sodom and Gomorrah were destroyed.
He'll find death, like Lot's wife, who tries most to avoid.

Where two in their bed lie or out at the mill grind,
One will be taken and the other left behind.

Make sure that you in God's good graces stay,
As you know not the hour nor the day."

224 The Parable of the Good Servant and the Wicked Servant
Mt. 24:45-51, Lk. 12:41-46

"Who is the servant, both faithful and wise,
And worthy to dominion exercise?

His master leaves him to the household feed.
Blest is that servant found doing his deed.

But woe will reach the wicked servant who
Decides, 'With him gone, I know what I'll do.'

He beats his fellow servants for his sport
And makes the foulest drunkards his consort.

The master will return when unexpected
And by the harshest means he'll be corrected.

That servant will be kicked and whipped, thrown out like trash,
Where tears will flow like rivers and his teeth will gnash.

Who knows his master's will, and yet does not adhere,
Will get a beating well-deserved and most severe.

Who does not know and breaks his master's will
Shall bleed, but less, to discipline instill.

From those he grants much, much will be required.
The highest ranked can be the first one fired."

[312]

225 The Parable of the Ten Virgins
Mt. 25:1-13, Lk. 12:35-38

"The kingdom of the Lord's like virgins ten,
Who took their lamps to meet the bridegroom when

They heard he was approaching. Five were wise;
The others lacked the wit to realize

That lamps need oil for their light to keep.
When he was late, the ten all fell asleep

Then, after the delay, around midnight,
One of the ten awoke and soon caught sight,

'Hey, look! The bridegroom comes! Come out to meet!'
But five saw how their oil did deplete

Once they their lamps had trimmed. They asked those five,
'Can't you share some to keep our flames alive?'

They said, 'For both of us, we lack the store.
Just go to those who sell and get some more.'

And so left those without, the foolish five.
While gone, the bridegroom and the bride arrive.

The wise went in and then was shut the door.
Then entrance did the foolish five implore,

'Lord, let us come into your celebration.'
He said, 'Though you each had an invitation,

I saw you not. In truth I do not know you.
I cast you out and care not where you go to.'

Forsooth, I tell you, watchful always stay,
For you know not the hour nor the day."

226 The Parable of the Talents
Mt. 25:14-30, Lk. 19:11-27

"It's like a man who left to be made king,
Not wanting for to not earn anything.

He told his slaves, 'My money shan't gain dust.
To each a minor fortune I'll entrust.'

One servant got five talents, one got two,
The third just one, based on what each could do.

Some hateful servants sent a delegation
In order to prevent his coronation.

The first one traded his five in a way
That he had five more to the rich man pay.

The one with two, likewise, he earned two more,
While he with one under the ground did store.

When he returned, as king, he summoned those
So that their profits they could then disclose.

The first said, 'Five talents to me were given
And I was, out of loyalty, so driven

That five more have I earned. Please take them, lord.'
He said, 'Then you deserve a great reward!

Since you just proved yourself in things so small,
Some cities I will give you, ten in all,

To govern them. Thus will I your talents employ.
Now come with me and you shall share your master's joy.'

The second said, 'I, too, have doubled mine!'
'That's great! Then in like ways shall I assign.

Some cities shall you govern. Five, no less.
You, too, shall share your master's happiness.'

At last, it was the final servant's turn,
Who said, 'Sir, I know you're a master stern,

Reaping where you've not sown, likewise you gather
Where you've not scattered. So I thought I'd rather

Just bury what you gave me in the ground.
Don't worry. What I thought misplaced I found.[188]

[316]

So here it is.' 'You wicked, worthless fool!
Unlike the others, nothing shall you rule.

Again you've shown what truly is your worth.
To hide a talent underneath the earth!

You could have placed it in a bank, at least.
With interest, then, my wealth would have increased.

You have condemned yourself by what you've known.
'Tis true I'm one who reaps where I've not sown.'

And then he said unto his hired men,
'Give his talent to him who now has ten.

For he who has will keep receiving more,
And those without will grow forever poor.

Throw him into the darkness where he'll find
Nothing but weeping eyes and teeth that grind.

And as for those who sent the delegation,
I'll see them killed for insubordination.'"

227 The Final Judgment
Mt. 25:31-46

"The Son of Man shall come, enthroned in glory,
To judge those from each land and territory,

With angels 'round Him, in rows hundreds deep,
To sort mankind, as goats are rent from sheep.

He'll place goats on His left, sheep on his right,
And tell the sheep, with eyes filled with delight,

'Come to My Father's kingdom, you most blessed,
For whom God made a place for you to rest.

For God can outdo all in gratitude.
You saw Me hungry and you gave Me food.

You saw Me thirsty and My thirst relieved,
And from you needed shelter was received.

You welcomed Me when I trod in a foreign land.
When I laid sick in bed, you held onto My hand.

You even came to visit when in prison.
Come live the life the Lord made for the risen!'

The righteous then will ask this of their Lord,
'When did we give what You could not afford?

When did we visit You, in sickbed or in jail?
When did we house You when You walked a foreign trail,

[318]

Or give you clothes, not that we want to disagree?'
'What's done for the least of My brethren's done for Me.'

Then those placed on His left side will be cursed,
'Be gone, for fates are only once reversed!

For I was hungry, but you gave no food,
A stranger far from home and you were rude.

If naked, thirsty, locked in jail, or ill,
The aid that I received from you was nil.'

The wicked then will ask Him in reply,
'When did we charity for You deny?'

'If you let starve one single little child,[189]
You have the wrath of the Almighty riled.

To leave in need when help you can afford
Is to abandon and forsake your Lord.

To visit sick or those in jail you gave no time,
No matter how they suffered or had done no crime.

To foreigners, you cast them out as strangers,
To face the cold and any other dangers.

You passed the homeless with your pockets full.
You saw them cold and sold your excess wool.

They laid in rags, or naked as when they were born,
And they only received your laughter and your scorn.

For you cared not if God's children were cold,
If helping them meant lessening your gold.

What crime is worse, when wanting to your wealth maintain,
Than letting children in hunger and thirst remain?

As thirsty as kids were, you let them thirst,
With bellies swollen like they soon could burst.

You saw their need and did not do a thing,
And so deserve eternal suffering.

You'll burn in blazing flames throughout an endless age,'
He'll tell these selfish people, with eyes filled with rage.

They will be sent to the eternal fire,
While selfless folk join God's angelic choir."

228 Jesus Teaches in Jerusalem
Lk. 21:37-38

In these days, Christ would in the Temple teach,
Where vast crowds gathered for to hear His speech.

Then at the Mount of Olives Jesus stayed,
Where He took rest and to the Father prayed.

229 Greeks Seek Jesus and Hear of His Death
Jn. 12:20-36

Now, at the festival, some who were Greek,
Came up to Philip, "Your master we seek."

So Philip, as he knew not their intention,
Went after Andrew to their purpose mention.

So they went and told Jesus, who replied,
"The hour when the Son is glorified,

In truth I tell you, it is now arrived.
No seed bears fruit, as long as it survived.

Lest grains of wheat fall to the earth and die,
They stay the same and cannot multiply.

Yet when it dies, a rich harvest is yielded.
Now anyone who would from death be shielded

Will lose his life, while he willing to sacrifice
Will gain eternal life, who paid the highest price.

The one who serves Me follows Me as well
And, in return, will dwell where I will dwell.

My Father will grant My servants reward.
What can I tell Him? I cannot afford

To suffer what I came to earth to do?
My heart aches knowing what I must go through.

Please, Father, through Me glorify Your name."
"I have, and I again will do the same,"

A voice from heaven said, stunning the crowd.
Some thought it angels, some thunder most loud.

"It's not for My sake that you heard this voice,
But for your sake, that you make the right choice.

Unto this world shall judgment soon be passed,
And then the prince of this world shall not last.

When I am lifted from the earth shall I
Draw everyone to where I dwell on high."

Yet this prediction of His crucifixion
Was met by, "Is this not a contradiction?

It's said, 'The Christ forever will remain.'
Yet that the Son be raised up you maintain.

Then tell us who this Son of Man could be."
"The light will not long stay that you might see.

Go on your way while still among you is the light.
For men cannot, without illuminated sight,

Know where they go and overtake them darkness will.
So put faith in the light while it is with you still.

Then children of the light you might become,"
He said to those He then was hidden from.

230 The Unbelief of the People
Jn. 12:37-43

Although they'd seen performed by Him many a sign,
They had not faith in Him, and this was all in line

With what Isaiah said, "Lord, who heard our report?
Who knew I spread Your word and never did distort?"[190]

They were faithless for, as Isaiah said,
"He has made blind the two eyes in your head

And, in addition to this, He's made hard your heart
So you use not these organs, but another part.

When these both fail, with these organs unfeeling,
Then they shall learn and turn to God for healing.'[191]

He said these, having seen the glory of the Lord
And told how the Messiah would meet their discord."

Now many, even leaders, did believe,
But chose not to admit it, but deceive,

For fear of Pharisees and the synagogue ban,[192]
Preferring to God's glory the glory of man.

231 Judgment by the Word
Jn. 12:44-50

So Christ declared, "He who believes in Me also
Believes the one who said that I to you must go.

Who sees Me sees the one who sent Me here.
I came as light so men's sight be made clear,

That those with faith in Me darkness avoid.
Who hears My words and only gets annoyed,

And does not faithfully hold true to them,
It is not I that shall this man condemn.

I came not to condemn men, but to save.
Who hears My words and does not thus behave

Already stands condemned against My word.
The evidence shall be the truth you heard.

For I've not spoken of My own accord,
But have relayed the message of the Lord,

Which gives eternal life to those who seek.
Hence all He told Me is all that I speak."

Chapter XIV
The Last Supper

232 Jesus Foretells His Death
Mt. 26:1-5, Mk. 14:1-2, Lk. 22:1-2

Now, after this, to His disciples Jesus said,
"In two days comes the feast where blood of lambs is shed,

Where I shall be delivered to be crucified."

233 Judas Conspires with the Chief Priests
Mt. 26:14-16, Mk. 14:10-11, Lk. 22:3-6

At the palace of the high priest, gathered inside,

The elders and chief priests together planned
By what deceit they would Christ's life demand.

They feared the people and on this agreed,
"We must not do this at the feast." "Indeed."

Judas Iscariot by Satan was enticed,
And sought the chief priests, "How high is my teacher priced?"

They shook, that thirty silver pieces they would pay,
And Judas sought a means by which he would betray.

234 The Disciples Prepare the Passover Feast
Mt. 26:17-20, Mk. 14:12-17, Lk. 22:7-14

Then came the first day of Unleavened Bread,
When blood of the Passover lamb is shed.

So His disciples questioned Christ on where
They were to the Passover feast prepare.

"On entering the city, you will meet
One with a jar of water on the street.

Just follow him and unto the householder say,
'The Teacher asks, "Where is the room in which we'll stay,

Where Passover would well be celebrated?"'
Then in a room will you be situated,

An upper room with couches lying all around."
So John and Peter went, and all He said was found.

All was prepared, as best as they were able,
And that night Jesus joined the twelve at table.

235 Washing the Disciples' Feet
Jn. 13:1-20

At night, Christ thought how He would miss His every friend,
And knew that He had loved them all, right through the end.

Now Judas had by Satan been inspired
To sell Christ for the silver he desired.

Christ knew that, as from Heaven He was sent,
When from His close disciples He was rent,

Then with His Father He'd be reunited.
The twelve were each in front of Him invited.

He washed their feet and thus a servant's role embraced,
And wiped them with the towel wrapped around His waist,

After His outer garment was removed.
When it was his turn, Peter disapproved.

"My Lord, do You really intend to wash my feet?"
"Your understanding will at one time be complete."

"I will not have You kneel like you're enslaved!"
"If I don't wash you, you will not be saved."

"Well, then, Lord, wash my hands and head as well!"
"One who has bathed is clean and does not smell,

Save for the feet, since they walk on the ground.
Yet one of you will not so clean be found."

When finished washing all their feet by hand,
He asked, "Do you My action understand?

You call Me Lord and Master, rightly so,
But what is this if My ways you don't know?

Just as you all have seen Me wash your feet,
This action you must, one and all, repeat.

For, just as any master is above his slave,
No messenger outranks him who the message gave.

So blest are you if you believe in such a way,
But I do not mean all. For does not Scripture say,

'Who shares my table treats me with malignity.'?[193]
I foretell this so you will know that I am He.

In truth, whoever welcomes one that I will send
Welcomes Myself and Him who sent Me, in the end."

236 The Last Supper
Mt. 26:26-29, Mk. 14:22-25, Lk. 22:15-20

Then Jesus said, "I've ardently desired,
Before My cruel betrayal has transpired,

To share this meal with you, for I'll not eat again,
Until it is fulfilled, not in the world of men."

As they were eating, Jesus took some bread.
He blessed it, broke it, gave it out and said,

"Take, eat. This is My Body, given up for you.
In memory of Me, the same thing you shall do."

He took the cup and, after thanks was given,
Declared, "In order that sins be forgiven,

Drink this, for this cup is My Blood, which shall be poured,
And shall be the new covenant, sent from the Lord.

I shall not drink of the fruit of the vine
'Till in My Father's kingdom we all dine."

237 Jesus Foretells His Betrayal
Mt. 26:21-25, Mk. 14:18-21, Lk. 22:21-23, Jn. 13:21-30

Then Jesus, most deeply disturbed, declared,
"Soon one of you, for whom I've always cared,

Shall double-cross Me." So they looked around,
And waited, hoping Jesus would expound.

"Surely, it's not I." "Who would be so devilish?"
"This curséd one is he who shares My dipping dish.

As it is written so the Son of Man must go,
Yet he who sends Him this way shall receive such woe.

He'd better be if never he existed."
"It surely is not I," Judas insisted.

"On your own word is this assertion based.
What you intend to do, just do with haste."

Now no one sitting there could understand
Why Jesus gave to Judas this command.

Since Judas held their money, they thought it was for
To buy food for the feast or give some to the poor.

Once Judas ate his morsel, he departed
And went out where the dark of night had started.

238 "Love One Another as I have Loved You"
Jn. 13:31-35

When he had gone, Christ said, "The Son's now glorified,
And in Him so is God. Now if I give Him pride,

Then God will glorify Me in Himself, and soon.
My little children, just as in late afternoon,

All know the sun will soon not be around,[194]
I'll leave, and if you look I'll not be found.

I must depart and, as I told the Jews,
You cannot follow, even should you choose.

I give a new command: to love each other,
Not just as if all were sister or brother,

But I will only count your love as ample
If you give love as I've given example.

For others shall know that you follow Me
When you love all of mankind boundlessly."

239 Jesus Predicts Peter's Denial
Mt. 26:30-35, Mk. 14:26-31, Lk. 22:31-34, Jn. 13:36-38

Then Jesus said, "Each one of you will fall away.
'I'll strike the shepherd and none of his flock will stay,'[195]

As it is written, and as you will see.
I'll go before you into Galilee,

All this once you witness that I have risen."
"I'd not abandon You if it meant prison,"

Insisted Peter, "Or it got me killed."
"This easy is to say before you're grilled.

You'll sell me out when hotter is the fire.
Had you but courage equal to desire![196]

This night before you hear the rooster crow
Three times will you deny the one you know.

For Satan has the chance to sift through you like wheat,
But I've prayed that you have the strength not to retreat.

When you betray Me and turn back again,
Help strengthen your fellow women and men."

"I won't deny you, even should I die."
So did all His disciples then reply.

240 The Two Swords
Lk. 22:35-38

Then Jesus asked, "When you were sent, sans shoes or purse,
Compared to when you had them, were you any worse?"

"No, Jesus, we were never then found lacking."
"This time I send you out I send you packing.

So bring your bag with what you can afford,
And if you lack one, go and buy a sword.[197]

For in Me will the Scriptures be fulfilled:
'When counted as a rebel, He was killed.'"

"Here are two swords, for when all things are rough."
Christ looked at them, declaring, "That's enough!"

[338]

241 "Let Not Your Hearts be Troubled"
Jn. 14:1-14

"Let not your hearts be troubled, but instead believe.
With faith, in Me and God, when from this world you leave,

You'll find I have prepared a place for you.
For I'd not promise what I could not do.

In truth, My Father's house has endless room,
More full of life and comfort than the womb.[198]

I will return when your place is prepared,
So that the kingdom might with you be shared.

You know the way to where I'll go and where we'll stay."
But Thomas said, "We don't. Where to and what's the way?"

Christ said, "I am the Way, the Truth, the Life.
As men gain children only through their wife,[199]

The Father's children only meet Him through His Son.
Through Me the revelation of the Father's done."

"Lord, show the Father and we shall be satisfied,"
Suggested Philip. "We have long walked side-by-side,"

Said Christ, "Yet even though His Son you've seen,
You act like He's hidden behind a screen.

For I have shown the Father's light, and no less dim.[200]
Don't you believe that He's in Me and I in him?

[339]

What I speak is not of My own accord,
But is the work of the almighty Lord.

You must believe that I'm in Him and He's in Me,
At least based on the evidence that you all see.

Those who believe will these same works perform,
And more, as shall your earthly task transform.

You'll do far more, with faith in Me and what I've taught,
For greater fish swim in the sea than have been caught.[201]

I'll be in Heaven and, what you ask in My name,
I'll grant it for the Father's glory to proclaim."

242 The Promise of the Paraclete
Jn. 14:15-26

"If you love Me, you will keep My command.
The Paraclete with you will always stand,

The Spirit of truth, whom I have the Father send,
With whom the world can neither know, see, nor be friend.

For as an orphan you will not be left,
Though you may sometimes feel as if bereft,

I will be with you though the world sees Me no more.
You'll see I live and live with Me forevermore.

On that day you'll know that in My Father I dwell,
And you will be in Me and I in you as well.

The ones who love Me hold true to My word;
On them My Father's love will be conferred,

And I will love them and reveal Myself to them."
The Judas who remained asked, "What's this stratagem?

How could You synchronously be to us revealed
And to the rest of the entire world concealed?"

"To those who love Me and from My path do not roam,
The Father will give love and in him make a home.

Who does not love Me does not keep My word,
And it was not My own message you heard,

But it comes from the Father, from whom I was sent.
When all My given time to spend with you is spent,

The Spirit whom the Father will send in My name
Will teach you all and help recall what I proclaim."

[341]

243 "Peace I Leave with You, My Peace I Give to You"
Jn. 14:27-31

"Shalom I grant you, deep peace from My heart,
A kind of peace the world cannot impart.

My friends, let not your hearts be troubled or afraid.
I shall return, as surely as I'll be betrayed.

If you loved Me, your songs of joy would amplify,
For I go to My Father, who's greater than I.

I've told you this, so when you doubt and grieve,
You'll know all I predicted and believe.

I will not long stay talking with you here,
As this world's prince will soon be drawing near.

He cannot beat Me, but the world must understand
I will submit to anything the Father planned,

Such love I leave Myself with no defense.
But let us rise, departing from here hence."

244 "I AM the True Vine"
Jn. 15:1-8

"I AM the vine, My Father the vinedresser,
Pruning greater branches, burning the lesser.

The branches that grow nothing are removed,
While those that bear fruit are trimmed and improved.

You have been pruned, by hearing what I've spoken.
You must remain in Me, a bond unbroken,

As I in you. As branches grow no fruit,
Unless fed by the vine, all through the root,

You'll bear no fruit if we are separated.
Yet they'll be endlessly reduplicated

If you're My branches and, in turn, I am your vine.
Apart you're like a plant sans water and sunshine.[202]

Then fruitless, you'll be cut off and decay
And thrown in furnaces when ends the day.

If you allow My words, like rain, to nourish,
From seed to forest shall your good works flourish."[203]

245 "Abide in My Love"
Jn. 15:9-17

"I've loved you as the Father has loved Me.
If you heed My commandments fervently,

Then shall you in My agape remain,
As are My Father and I, like a chain.[204]

I say this so you might see life as beautiful,
That you might have the joi de vie, that bliss in full.

My last command is love mankind as I've loved you.
No greater love is had, no greater can you do

Than sacrifice your very life up for a friend.
I do not call you servants, but My arms extend, [204]

Embracing you as friends, for I have told
What I heard from My Father to My fold. [204]

For servants do not know their master's will,
While I hid nothing that I could instill.

You chose Me not, but I chose and commissioned you,
That you bear many lasting fruits, not just a few.

Then will the Father give what you ask in My name.
As I have loved you, you must love all men the same."

246 The World's Hatred
Jn. 15:18-25

"If they hate you, it should be recognized
Before you were disliked I was despised.

If you were of this world, they'd love you as their own,
Yet this dark world I've called you from you have outgrown.[205]

As far as from this world you're separated,
Will you ascend and by this world be hated.

I've said, 'No slave is greater than his master.'
You can't avoid what looks like My disaster.[206]

As I am, so shall you be persecuted,
But your true vine will never be uprooted. [206]

If they had kept My word, they would keep yours.
But for My sake, you'll fall to carnivores

And even more horrendous roads you'll trod
Because the people do not know their God.

Had I not come, had they not heard all I proclaim,
Then for their wickedness they could receive no blame.

But, as they heard Me, they have no excuse.
When they oppress you, they bind their own noose. [207]

Had I not done works never done before,
Their lack of faith could be accounted for.

Despite all I have done for them to see,
They still despise both My Father and Me.

This will fulfill what's written in their laws,
'The people hated me without a cause.'"[208]

247 The Witness of the Paraclete
Jn. 15:26-27

"When comes to you the Paraclete, whom I shall send,
The Spirit true, which from the Father will descend,

He will bear witness of Me to all men.
You have been with Me since My work began

And shall be called upon to testify."

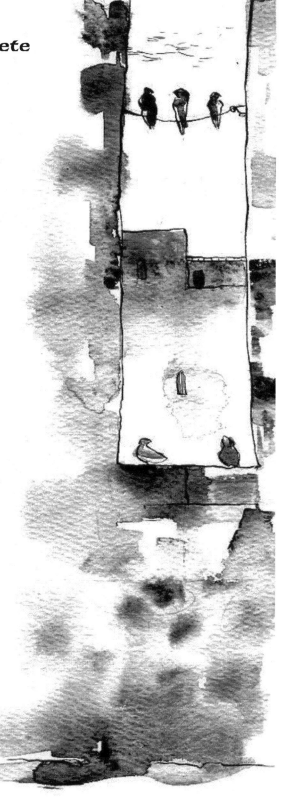

248 Upcoming Persecutions
Jn. 16:1-4

"I've said this so My words you'll not deny.

In truth, from synagogues you'll be expelled
Because the truth I told you you have held.

You'll see that those who bring death and discord
Will think they do a service to the Lord.

They'll do this since they know not My Father nor Me.
Then these words will be ingrained in your memory."

249 The Work of the Paraclete
Jn. 16:5-15

"Now, being here, I did not say these things before.
I go back to the Father, yet do you implore,

'Where are you going?' You just sulk in sorrow,
Afraid of what I said you'll meet tomorrow.

In truth, it is to your advantage that I leave
In order that the Advocate you may receive.

And when He comes, He'll show the world how much it erred,
How it was sinful and its judgment was impaired:

Concerning sin, that they would not believe;
Concerning righteousness, that I will leave,

Returning to the Father, to be seen no more;
On judgment, this world's prince has been condemned before.

I've much to say, of which you must be made aware,
But hearing all right now would be too much to bear.

Yet when the Spirit of truth comes to you,
Then you shall fully understand what's true,

For He will not speak of His own accord,
But shall speak what He is told by the Lord

And will reveal to you the things to come.
I will be glorified, for He speaks from

All that the Father has, which now I own,
For now He does not hold these things alone."

250 "Your Sorrow will Turn into Joy"
Jn. 16:16-22

"In a short time will I be from your eyes concealed,
But shortly after I'll be once again revealed."

Then His disciples asked, "What does He mean,
That in a short time He will not be seen?"

"What of this 'To the Father I'll return.'?"
"What of this 'short time' and all we must learn?"

Christ said, "I know you wonder what I meant,
Returning to the one by whom I'm sent.

In truth, in misery you'll raise your voices,
And while you mourn, you'll see the world rejoices.

Your crying shall turn into celebrating.
Though giving birth is so excruciating,

A mother's heart the world cannot contain,
Such that the mother can forget the pain

And, looking at her newborn girl or boy,
Be filled with such immeasurable joy.

It so shall be with you, though now depressed,
You shall see Me once you have passed the test

And, being with Me on that final day,
You'll have the joy that none can take away."

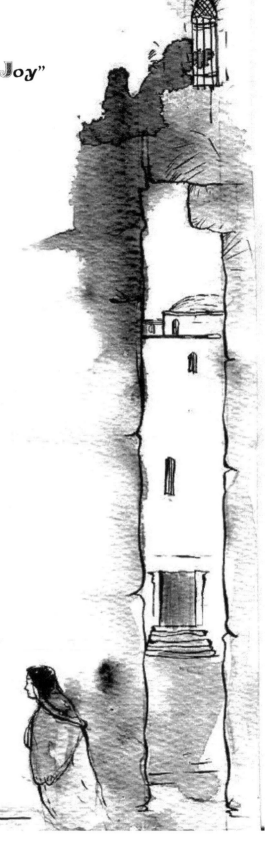

251 Prayer in the Name of Jesus
Jn. 16:23-28

"When comes that day, you'll not ask Me a question.
In truth, if you should follow My suggestion

And make requests to Yahweh in My name,
Your need and gift will surely be the same.

So far, you have not prayed in such a way.
You'll then receive what you ask when you pray

And you will know the joy that is complete.
My words have been symbolic and discreet.

My language won't be veiled in coming days,
But I shall teach you in the clearest ways.

When you pray to the Father in My name,
I need not ask that He give you the same,

For He will love you as you love His Son,
Believing the Father and I are one.

For I came from the Father to be here
And I shall in His midst soon reappear."

252 Prediction of the Disciples' Flight
Jn. 16:29-33

Said His disciples, "You are plainly speaking
And You know all the truth that we are seeking,

Not needing questions to be put before You.
Thus do we both believe in and adore You."

"Do you believe at last? The time will come to pass,
Or it has come, when you will run away en masse,

All leaving Me alone, yet I'll alone not be,
For anywhere I am the Father is with Me.

Now I have told you this, that peace may be with you.
Have courage, for you'll see how I the world subdue."

253 Jesus Prays to the Father for His Followers
Jn. 17:1-26

He raised His eyes up to the heavens to proclaim,
"When You will glorify Me You will gain acclaim,

Dear Father, for the hour now is here,
That I might give life to those who adhere,

As I was given power over all mankind.
That life is knowing Christ, who was to men assigned,

And knowing You, the only true God anywhere.
I have finished My Father's work, being His heir,

And, doing such, have given His due glory.
That men know Us in every territory,

Grant Me the glory I had with You when
I was with You before the world began.

I have revealed Your name and Your identity
To those You took out from the world and gave to Me.

For they were Yours and they have kept Your word,
And know that what I say from You I heard.

All that I have is given Me from You
And they know that what I teach them is true,

And that for Me and My words you're the source.
I pray for them, that they might stay the course.

I pray not for the world, but just for those,
The ones You gave to Me, the ones You chose.

All that I have is Yours, and Yours is Mine,
And through the ones You gave Me I will shine.

I leave the world to be with You, but they remain.
Help those You gave Me keep Your words when they must strain,

In order that they be united, as We are.
While on My watch, none of My sheep have wandered far,

Save one of them, who is so badly lost
He knows not where his road goes nor its cost.

He gave himself to evil; thus his soul was killed,
But through his actions will the scriptures be fulfilled.

I told Your children how I will return above
That they have joy, and hope in Him I teach them of.

I taught them and by this world they were hated.
Like Me, they and the world are separated.

You need not take them from where they rejected,
But keep them from the Evil One protected.

For they are Yours and no more in the world than I,
So consecrate them in the truth they'll prophesy.

As You have sent Me to this world, I send them, too.
And for their sake, I dedicate Myself to you,

That they be consecrated in the truth as well.
I also pray for those who they the good news tell,

Who through their words come to believe in Me.
As we have, may they share such unity.

As You and I both in each other dwell,
May all those faithful live in Us as well,

That they might show the world most evidently
My nature and that of the one who sent Me.

I've shared My glory, with My truth and clarity,
That they might be as one, in solidarity.

With Us in them, with our fire ignited,[209]
May they all be as perfectly united,

That through their union all will recognize
How much You love, care for, and empathize.

[354]

Please grant that those who have to Me been given
Might always be with Me when I am risen,

That they might see My glory in My station
You gave Me out of love before creation.

For this world has not known You, as have I,
And I told them who I was sent here by.

I have made known Your name, and always will do so,
That, in Us, with Our love, they hardships undergo."

Chapter XV
Jesus is Brought to Trial

254 The Garden at Gethsemane
Mt. 26:36-46, Mk. 14:32-42, Lk. 22:39-46, Jn. 18:1

Once they together sang a hymn of prayer, they went
Into Gethsemane, where Jesus could lament.

So Christ asked that they in the garden stay:
"Sit here, while I go further on to pray,

But where I go I wish to take with Me
Both Peter and the sons of Zebedee.[210] "

There He was filled with great distress and sorrow,
Anticipating all He'd bear that morrow.

 "At near the point of death do I feel misery.
Remain right here, together keeping watch with Me."

Then, going further, Jesus fell upon His face,
Imploring to avoid such pain and such disgrace.

"My Father, if it's possible, be it Your will,
Let this cup pass from Me, that I be saved from ill,

Yet not what My will is, but Yours be done."
Christ came to find them sleeping, every one.

He questioned Peter, "Why are you asleep?
Can you not simply one hour's watch keep?

Keep watch! And pray no evil things you do or speak!
The spirit may be willing, but the flesh is weak."

Again He went away from them and prayed,
As He had done before, beseeching aid.

"If this cup cannot pass unless I drink of it,
Then to Your faultless will I willingly submit."

Then Christ returned, to see how well the watch was kept,
To find that Peter, James and John most deeply slept.

"You see Me nearly dying from the tension
And you would rather dream than pay attention!"

Their eyes had shut, though to stand guard they tried,
And they knew not how they could have replied.

So He left for to pray for the third time,
Where, note for note, the same words He did chime.

When He returned, He said, "Are you still taking rest?
Behold, now is the hour where we meet our test,

Where most unrighteous men will reprimand.
Rise up, see My betrayer is at hand!"

255 The Arrest of Jesus
Mt. 26:47-56, Mk. 14:43-52, Lk. 22:47-53, Jn. 18:2-12

While He was speaking, there approached a crowd,
By Judas led, all violent and loud,

With clubs and swords, with chief priest, scribe and elder,
Who turned night's silence into helter-skelter.

They had a sign, "The one I kiss arrest."
So Judas kissed Christ, "Hail, Master, most blest!"

And Jesus stared him down, "You dare betray,
Using a kiss, a sign of agape?"

Then, facing them, "Who have you come to see?"
"Jesus the Nazarene!" "Well, I AM[211] He."

The crowd moved back and fell upon the ground.
"Whom do you seek?" He asked and looked around.

 "Jesus the Nazarene," they said again.
"Then why not leave untouched these other men?

For I AM He, as I have said to you before."
They asked their Christ, "Should we draw swords, like men at war?"

Before He could respond, Simon Peter came near,
Instantly cutting off the high priest's servant's ear.

 "Put that back! Who lives by the sword dies by the sword.
Don't you believe that if My Father I implored

Twelve legions would be instantly at My defense?
Yet this is how the Scriptures say it must commence."

Christ went to Malchus then, the injured slave,
And with His hand did that poor man's ear save.

He asked, "Why come as if a thief you sought?
I never hid a thing I did or taught.

I sat and taught at Temple every day,
And yet you never came in such a way.

Each day I taught there and was never grilled,
Yet all of this just makes Scriptures fulfilled."

His followers forsook Him then and fled.
A young man who just got out of his bed,

In just a linen cloth, was following behind.
They seized him, but he would not be in cloth confined.

[359]

256 Jesus is Brought before the Sanhedrin
Mt. 26:57-68, Mk. 14:53-65, Lk. 22:54-55, 53-71, Jn. 18:13-24

They brought Christ before Caiaphas, that year's high priest,
Who'd said the ministry of Christ must be surceased.

The chief priests, scribes and elders were assembled there,
While Peter was outside, as close as he could bare.

With him was a disciple by the high priest known,
Who had the way into the courtyard to them shown.

Now chief priests and the gathered council sought
Incriminating things that Jesus taught.

They first hoped damning evidence He'd volunteer.
"What I have taught I have pronounced for all to hear,

In synagogues and Temple, where all meet.
My words were not in secret or discreet.

Ask those who heard My words to make your case."
At this, one guard slapped Jesus in the face.

 "Is that the way You answer the high priest?!"
"If I offended, even in the least,

Bear witness to whatever wrong I said.
If not, why should you strike Me in the head?"

[360]

Though many came to lie and were insistent,
They had no case as lies were inconsistent.

Some said, "He claimed He'd tear the Temple to the ground
And in three days, just as it was, He'd have it found."

Yet, still, what they gave witness to did not agree.
The high priest questioned, "Have You no defense for me?

Will You not protest such an accusation?!"
His silence gave the high priest such frustration,

 "On oath before the living God I'll have you swear!
If You're the Christ, the Son of God, then so declare!"

Christ said, "It's you who have said this of Me.
But I tell you from this time you shall see

The Son of Man at the right hand of Power,
Come on heaven's clouds in the coming hour."

The high priest tore his robes in outrage and disgust.
"Convict this man of blasphemy we surely must!

Our witnesses need give no further word,
For what He has blasphemed we now have heard!

Shall He utter another from His breath?!"
The council answered, "No, He merits death!"

His face was covered, spat upon, punched in the eye,[212]
And all the time they taunted Him to prophesy,

 "Who struck You, Christ?! Tell us what You must know!
Who is it that dealt You the latest blow?!"

257 Peter's Denial
Mt. 26:69-75, Mk. 14:66-72, Lk. 22:56-62, Jn. 18:25-27

While Peter warmed himself, outside where fires burned,
The maid who let him in in his direction turned,

"This man right here was with the Nazarene."
But Peter said, "This man I have not seen."

Though he went to the porch, after a while,
Another, seeming to put him on trial,

Proclaimed, "You're one of them! It's clear to see.
Your accent shows you hail from Galilee."

Yet Peter still protested, "That's not so!
I'm from there, but this man I do not know."

A kin of Malchus later came, "You're in His lot!
Did you think your face from the garden I forgot?"

Peter invoked a curse upon himself and swore,
"I do not know this man and never have before!"

Then, instantly, they heard the rooster crow
And Peter felt like dealt with a deathblow.

For then did he recall Jesus' word,
"Before the crowing of the rooster's heard,

You will deny that you have even known Me thrice."
He broke down, crying, that his heart did not suffice.

258 Jesus is Delivered to Pilate
Mt. 27:1-2, Mk. 15:1, Lk. 23:1, Jn. 18:28

Now when the morning came, the council met
To get a condemnation from their threat.

So they had Jesus bound and led away
To Pilate, who could execute or stay.

259 The Death of Judas[213][1]
Mt. 27:3-10

On seeing that condemned now stood his Lord,
By such remorse and guilt was Judas floored.

He took the silver back to those who paid,
"I've sinned! It's innocent blood I betrayed!"

They asked him, "What is that to us? That's your concern."
Then Judas threw the silver to his fee return.

Into the sanctuary went his ill-got pelf
And Judas ran in bitter tears and hung himself.

They asked, "What shall we do, for as goes the precept,
Blood money cannot in the treasury be kept."

They took the coins and bought the potter's field,
Just meant for graves for foreigners to yield.

Therefore by "Field of Blood" this land was long referred.
This all fulfilled the holy prophet's ancient word,

"The thirty silver pieces the Jews took,
Wealth for which they the precious one forsook,

They used it for to buy the potter's field,
As God directed me, as He revealed."[214]

260 The Trial before Pilate
Mt. 27:11-14, Mk. 15:2-5, Lk. 23:2-5, Jn. 18:29-38

So Pilate went to them, "What accusation
Has you approach me for His condemnation?"

"If dreadful evil this man did not do,
Then we would not have handed Him to you."

"Then by your laws shall you this man accuse."
"But Rome won't let us execution use."

Now this was done in order to fulfill
How Jesus had foretold His blood would spill.

"By Him men are to revolution driven,
Told tribute cannot be to Caesar given,

And the most sinful, revolutionary thing
Is claiming to be Christ, God's sole anointed king."

So Pilot went to Him, "Are You king of the Jews?"
"Do you ask this, or did some others this term use?"

"Think You I am a Jew? It's Your own nation
That handed You to me for condemnation.

Tell me what sin or treason You committed."
"My kingdom is not one for this world fitted.

If it were here, would not My servants fight?
Would not they, for My sake, the crowds incite?

In truth, the kingship I have does not come from here."
"So you're a king?" "You've said so and I do appear

For this, and so that truth be widely known.
The true ones hear My voice and them alone."

He scoffed at Jesus, "Truth? And what is this?"
Yet Christ spoke not their charges to dismiss.

 "Have You not heard all that's been testified?!
Will not You even say they all have lied?"

Since Jesus would not offer a defense,
Pilate was filled with wonder most immense.

So Pilate told the chief priests and the crowd,
"This man did nothing Rome has disallowed."

But they insisted, "He spreads insurrection
All over and you'll not give Him correction?"

261 Jesus is brought Before Herod
Lk. 23:6-12

Then Pilate asked, "Is He from Galilee?"
And since He was, "Then Herod He shall see."

For Galilee was Herod's jurisdiction,
And Pilate sought to dodge religious friction.

He was around for the Passover feast,
So Christ was into Herod's hands released.

Now seeing Christ gave Herod such delight,
Who long wished to have Jesus in his sight,

Mostly to see a miracle performed.
Though questioned, Christ would not leave him informed.

While priests and scribes there pressed their accusation,
His silence once again gave them frustration.

So Herod and his guards gave Him contempt and scorn,
And sent Him in a cloak meant to by kings be worn.

Though Herod had been Pilate's hated rival,
On this day did these leaders reconcile.

262 Pilate Declares Jesus Innocent
Lk. 23:13-16

Then Pilate summoned priests and leading men,
"Though you accused, I say to you again,

While you claim by Him crowds were agitated,
A charge I have deeply investigated,

No grounds exist to have Him killed or stay interned,
And Herod thinks the same, for He has been returned.

He has done naught to crucifixion undergo,
So I shall have Him flogged and then will let Him go."

263 Jesus or Barabbas?
Mt. 27:15-23, Mk. 15:6-14, Lk. 23:17-23, Jn. 18:39-40

Now it was a tradition at the feast
The Jews could have one prisoner released.

One man in prison had such notoriety
That none should want him living in society.

When came the crowd, all seeking a release,
Then Pilate thought he could this nuisance cease.

 "Barabbas, who revolted and a man's throat sliced,[215]
Or give you Jesus, who is also known as Christ?"

For Christ was brought there out of envy, he perceived,
Not that He broke a law, nor that this was believed.

And Pilate had been sent word from his wife,
"Have naught to do with taking this man's life.

I tell you with all certainty that He's upright,
Since dreams about Him haunted me all yesternight."

The chief priests and the elders stirred the crowd,
"Release Barabbas!" they all screamed most loud.

So Pilate asked, "Then how should I my judgment use
In dealing with the one you call King of the Jews?"

In unison, all those assembled cried,
"Away with Him and have Him crucified!"

 "Why kill this man? What evil has He done?
I looked for proof of misdeeds and found none.

But I will have Him whipped before released."
Yet cries made by the crowds could not be ceased.

264 "Behold the Man!"
Mt. 27:27-31a, Mk. 15:16-20a, Jn. 19:1-15

Then Jesus was inside the palace led away,
Where gathered a battalion to keep crowds at bay.

First Pilate had the Christ severely whipped.
Then, by the guards, of His clothes He was stripped,

And they were substituted by a purple cloak.
They made a crown of thorns for to complete their joke.

With just as much contempt as they could use,
They knelt down, laughing, "Hail, King of the Jews!"

They spat upon Him and, taking the reed,
Struck His head where their sharp thorns made Him bleed.

Once finished with their game and their attack,
They stripped Him once more, giving His clothes back.

Then Pilate went out, "I bring Him here one more time
That you may know that I have found in Him no crime."

Christ came outside, where blood down His face ran,
And Pilate said to them, "Behold the man!"

The guards and chief priests saw and made a cry,
"Crucify the man! You must crucify!"

"Do this yourselves, for no crime has He done!"
"This man has made Himself to be God's Son,

And by our law this means that He must die!"
"That's why we said that you must crucify!"

These latest words made Pilate all the more afraid.
He questioned Christ again, but no response was made.

"Why in the world would You not speak to me?
For I could have You killed or set You free!"

"You would not have the power you so love
Were it not given to you from above;

Hence, those who sent Me here to you bear greater blame."
Though Pilate sought to free Him, Jews then made the claim,

"If you release this man, you are not Caesar's friend.
If someone makes Himself king, how can you defend?"

So Pilate took Christ to the judgment seat,
At Gabbatha, where to reduce the heat,

He ridiculed the gathered crowd,[216] "Behold your king!"
"He's a pretender, not the king of anything!

Take Him out to be killed!" "Your own king you would stone?"
The chief priests said, "Our only king holds Caesar's throne."

265 Pilate Washes his Hands and Delivers Jesus to be Crucified
Mt. 27:24-26, Mk. 15:15, Lk. 23:24-25, Jn. 19:16

When Pilate saw that forming was a riot,
He knew just one thing would the masses quiet.

They cried, "This man must on a cross be nailed!"
So, in the end, the rule of mob prevailed.

Reluctantly, he heeded their demands,
But Pilate first before them washed his hands.

"I'm innocent of this man's blood. It's your concern."
"Responsibility for it we will not spurn.

Let His blood be on us and our children as well."[217]
So Pilate had Barabbas released from his cell,

Despite the murder and revolt conviction,
And handed Jesus up for crucifixion.

266 The Road to Golgotha
Mt. 27:31b-32, Mk. 15:20b-21, Lk. 23:26-32, Jn. 19:17a

They led Him out, compelling Simon of Cyrene
To help Him, as His hardship easily was seen,

Though he was just a man there from the countryside.
Christ could not die before He could be crucified.[218]

A crowd then followed Him, whose wish had not prevailed,
Among whom many women mourned and loudly wailed.

 "Oh, Daughters of Jerusalem, don't weep for Me,
But rather for yourselves and for your family.

For days are coming when it will be said,
'Blest be the ones who have not children fed,

Whose wombs are barren and whose breasts have never nursed!
For those with little children have been truly cursed!'

The folks will beg the mountains, 'Please, upon us fall!!'
And 'Cover us!!' the hills, such terror will fill all.

If this befalls green wood, what happens when it's dry?"
Then all the more did heartfelt tears fill every eye.

[374]

267 The Crucifixion
Mt. 27:33-37, Mk. 15:22-26, Lk. 23:33-34, 38, Jn. 19:17b-27

When they reached Golgotha, which was its Hebrew name,
Called Calvary by Romans, though this meant the same,

"The place of a skull", women offered wine with myrrh,
Which could, when under great distress the senses blur.

He turned it down, which none could understand.
They laid Him down, then grabbed Him by the hand,

And hammered through it with a nail immense,
Which gave such pain, so viciously intense,

Such hurt that's rarely felt outside of hell.
His other hand and feet were pierced as well.

The cross was lifted and implanted in the ground,
And nailed-through hands and feet supported every pound.

To their great shock He said, despite what He went through,
"Forgive them, Father, for they know not what they do."

Now Pilate had the charge placed overhead,
In Hebrew, Greek, and Latin, and it read,

"Jesus of Nazareth, King of the Jews."
The chief priests said, "Other words you should use.

Put not 'King of the Jews', but write instead,
'"I am the king of all Jews," this man said.'"

But Pilate just responded, "What I wrote I wrote."
And, being near the city, many read the quote.

Now, while He hung there, dying on a cross,
The soldiers sought to profit from His loss.

The soldiers who had crucified Him numbered four,
So into four pieces these men His garments tore.

And, as His tunic had without a seam been sewn,
One said, "Let us cast lots so one of us can own!"

This all fulfilled exactly what the Scripture shows,
"They'll split my garments and they'll cast lots for my clothes."[219]

For His disciples this was all too scary,
But there were many near Him known as Mary:

The mother of both James, as well as Joseph,
Mary Magdalene and the wife of Clopas.

His mother stood there close by, most importantly,
Beside her sister and the wife of Zebedee.

With His beloved disciple and mother there,
He said, "Woman, this is your son. That is My prayer."

And, turning, said, "She's your mother as well."
Then, after, to his house she went to dwell.

268 Jesus is Derided on the Cross
Mt. 27:38-43, Mk. 15:27-32a, Lk. 23:35-37

Right next to Jesus had been crucified
Two criminals, one placed on either side.

The people passing by stopped there to criticize,
"You said the Temple You could knock down and make rise.

So save Yourself! If you're God's Son, get off Your cross!"
The chief priests laughed, "Look at the king! Look at the boss!"

"Did He not save people from everywhere?
Yet He cannot get Himself down from there!"

"Will not our king from this hardship Himself relieve?
If He did this, then we would all see and believe!"

"Let God deliver Him if He's the Chosen One!
For He has said, 'I trust in God. I am His Son.'"

269 The Two Thieves
Mt. 27:44, Mk. 15:32b, Lk. 23:39-43

Then did one hanging there insults at Jesus yell,
"Are you not Christ? Then save Yourself and us as well!"

The other then rebuked him, "How dare you such gall!
Do you have no fear of almighty God at all?

By all of us the same sentence was served,
But we have gotten what we have deserved.

He suffers here with us although He did no sin.
Remember me, Lord when Your kingship You begin."

So Jesus said, "In truth, as you regret your vice,
This very day you will join Me in paradise."

270 The Death of Jesus
Mt. 27:45-54, Mk. 15:33-39, Lk. 23:44-48, Jn. 19:28-30

At the sixth hour, darkness covered all the land,
Until the ninth, like light was covered by God's hand.[220]

Christ "Eli, Eli, lama sabachthani?" cried,
Which means, "My God, My God, why've You cast me aside?"[221]

Now they misheard Him, those who His words reached,
"Behold! Elijah He has just beseeched!"

His words were hard to understand, His throat so dry,
And, on the verge of death, He said, "Thirsty am I."

One ran, taking a sponge, sticking through it a reed,
Dunked it in vinegar and satisfied His need.

Yet others told him, "Wait and let us see
Whether Elijah comes to set Him free."

He loudly cried out, "Father, to Your hands do I
Commit My spirit!" Then to those who stood nearby,

"It is finished," He told them with His final breath.
In this manner did Jesus Christ succumb to death.

The curtain of the Temple, then, was torn in two,
The earth shook violently, and rocks were split right through.

When the centurion saw chaos and uproar,
He said, "That this man is God's Son we can be sure."

As for those in the crowd, who saw the world's unrest,
Each one returned home, fearfully, and beat their breast.

Some women watched this, who had known Him through the years,
Together mourning, wailing, overcome with tears.

271 Soldiers Pierce Jesus' Side
Jn. 19:31-37

Since fast approaching was the Sabbath day,
The Jews said on a cross they could not stay.

They asked that legs be broken, so that without breath,[222]
The three men crucified would then succumb to death.

The soldiers broke the legs of those on either side,
But when they came to Christ, they saw that He had died.

They did not break His legs, but pierced His side instead,
And instantly poured water and more blood was shed.[223]

In truth, eyewitnesses have these words spoken.
And Scripture told, "His bones will not be broken." [224]

Again it was by the Scriptures predicted,
"You'll look on him with spear you have inflicted."[225]

272 The Burial of Jesus
Mt. 27:57-61, Mk. 15:42-47, Lk. 23:50-56, Jn. 19:38-42

Then came forth Joseph of Arimathea,
A member of the council in Judea,

A good and righteous man of great respect,
Who did the chance to join their plot reject.

He was a man who ardently the kingdom sought,
Who secretly believed the things that Jesus taught.

He'd kept his faith in Jesus Christ concealed
For fear what Jews might do were it revealed.

Now Joseph asked the body be to him released,
And Pilate verified first Jesus was deceased.

When the centurion this fact relayed,
The lifeless corpse in Joseph's arms was laid.

With him was Nichodemus, who first came at night,
Now bearing myrrh and aloes, now in public sight,

So much about a hundred pounds the spices weighed.
With these, and in a linen shroud, the corpse was laid.

They placed Him in a tomb, one that was freshly hewn,
And never used, while ending was the afternoon.

So all the crowds into their homes retired,
That they might rest, as Sabbath law required.

273 The Guard at the Tomb
Mt. 27:62-66

The next day the chief priests and Pharisees
Sought Pilate, "Our governor if you please,

We now recall when Jesus was alive,
He claimed that execution He'd survive.

'When comes the third day, I will rise again.'
Therefore, secure His tomb with many men.

It must be kept secure through the third day,
Lest His disciples steal the corpse away.

If they then say, 'He's risen from the dead,'
This fraud will be the worst one they have said."

Said Pilate, "You have guards. Secure it as you can."
So they sealed shut the stone and put in place their men.

Chapter XVI
The Son Rises and the
Church Receives the Spirit

274 The Women at the Tomb [226]
Mt. 28:1-8, Mk. 16:1-8, Lk. 24:1-12, Jn. 20:1-13

Then visited the tomb, when passed the Sabbath day,
Joanna, Mary Magdalene, and Salome,

Mary, James' mother, and other women who
Had witnessed what Christ taught and what He just went through.

Still on their way, they wondered, "Who will move the stone?"
The earth then shook, where many things were split and thrown,

Which left the guards unconscious on the ground.[227]
The women dropped their spices when they found

The stone rolled back and barren laid the tomb.
They knew not what they should from this assume.

So Mary Magdalene left with the greatest speed
To tell the others and see how they should proceed.

Those who remained were met by angels two,
Whose robes were like the sun-lit snow to view,

Who looked like lightning not to this world bound.
In fear, they bowed their faces to the ground.

"Fear not. For you seek Jesus, who was crucified.
Why seek the one who lives among those who have died?

He is not here! For He has risen, as He said!
Look where He lay! You do not see a body dead!

Recall He said He'd suffer under sinful men,
Be crucified, but on the third day rise again."

They comprehended then every prediction,
How He would rise after His crucifixion.

"So do not stand here pondering. Make haste!
The sorrow felt must be with hope replaced![228]

[384]

Tell Peter and the others of this joyful news!
And He will meet them, that belief they can't refuse."

Like Mary, quickly as they could they fled
To tell them Jesus was no longer dead.

Now Mary Magdalene reached the disciples first,
So out of breath she felt as if her lungs could burst.

"They took His body and we know not where it's placed!
You must come with me now! My path must be retraced!"

So the beloved disciple and Peter, too
Rushed to the tomb to verify that this was true.[229]

At first, the two were running side-by-side,
But Peter could not match the other's stride.

Arriving first, he stayed outside and saw the shroud:
That Peter be the first to see it he allowed.

So Peter came into the tomb and found
It empty, save the cloth left on the ground.

The other entered then and instantly believed.
They understood those words before His death received.

Then did these two the sense of Scripture learn
And in awe did they to their homes return.

Now Mary Magdalene was near the tomb and wept.
She turned to look once more at where the corpse was kept.

She saw two angels there, as white as any sheep,
Who asked her, "Lady, why do you so sorely weep?"

"My Lord was laid here and they've taken Him away.
I know not where, for I came to anoint today."

She turned then and saw Christ, but did not recognize.
"My lady, what loss left so filled with tears your eyes?"

That this was just the gardener there she believed.
"If you moved Him, say where, that He may be retrieved."

He used His voice, as altered were His features,
"Mary!" "Rabboni!" (a term used for teachers)

"That you should hold Me I did not intend;
I did not yet to My Father ascend.

Depart and find the brethren, making sure they know
To My Father and theirs, to our God I go."

She told all the disciples, "I have seen the Lord!"
Relaying all He said and their hope was restored.

275 Jesus Appears to the Women
Mt. 28:9-10, Mk. 16:9-11, Jn. 20:14-18

While running back, the other women stopped and saw
The risen Christ, who greeted "Hail!" to their great awe.

They bowed down, grabbed His feet, and gave Him praise.
So Christ assured, "Abandon fearful ways.

Go find and tell the brethren everything you see,
That I have risen and soon head for Galilee."

276 The False Report of the Guard
Mt. 28:11-15

Some guards reported to the chief priests what took place,
So they assembled, plotting how they could save face.

They gave the soldiers money to the secret keep.
"Tell all that it was stolen while you were asleep.

Should Pilate hear this, we'll keep you protected."
And this lie spread, since they did as directed.

277 The Road to Emmaus
Lk. 24:13-35

On the road to Emmaus, later on that day,
Two followers were walking, talking on their way,

Discussing all the things that had occurred,
The things they witnessed and the news they heard.

Then Christ walked with them, but they did not recognize,
Because prevented from this knowledge were their eyes.

He asked, "What speak you of, that seems so deep?"
They stopped and looked at Him, like they could weep.

Asked Cleopas, "Could You not know? Did no one tell?
We thought all people knew what in these days befell."

He asked, "What happened?" "Well, Jesus the Nazarene,
A mighty prophet before God and people seen,

A man whose strong words were with mighty deeds applied,
By our chief priests was He condemned and crucified.

We hoped He'd be the one to set our country free."
"And that's not all. Some women from our company[230]

This very morning went to see His tomb
For to anoint with spices and perfume.

[389]

They found an empty tomb when they arrived!"
"Surely the cross He could not have survived!"[231]

"And angels then appeared to them and said
This Jesus had been risen from the dead!

Some friends of ours went to the tomb and found
It empty save the cloth laid on the ground.

Yet of this prophet they found not a trace."
Christ said, "You foolish men, quicken your pace!

Your hopes are headed in the wrong direction.
The Christ came not to help with insurrection![232]

So slowly men believe what prophets said!
Must not the Christ die and rise from the dead,

Before He enters His eternal glory?"
Christ traced as far back as Moses' story,

Through Elijah, Isaiah, Jeremiah,
And others, how they spoke of the Messiah.

It seemed like more time walking He'd be spending,
So they told Christ, "The day will soon be ending.

Come eat with us, and You may spend the night."
Jesus accepted and, before their sight,

He took the bread and over it a blessing said.
Then Jesus broke it and He gave to them the bread.

[390]

In this one action opened were their eyes.
They now their risen Christ could recognize.

Though they were filled with such boundless delight,
He instantly had vanished from their sight.

They said, "As He taught Scripture, did not our hearts burn?"
"And how much did we to comprehend further yearn?"

They instantly ran back on that same road
And felt the news they carried could explode.

They came to the eleven and some friends,
Who said, "He's risen and He soon ascends,

And was this very day by Simon Peter seen!"
The two told how they walked with Jesus in between,

How He made understood what Scripture said
And how they knew Him when He broke the bread.

278 Jesus Appears to His Disciples (Thomas being Absent)
Lk. 24:36-43, Jn. 20:19-23

As they together hid with their doors locked that night,
For thoughts that Jews would kill them, too, filled them with fright,

Christ came and stood with them, "Peace be with you,"
He said with hands and feet plainly in view.

"Why are your hearts so full of fear and doubt?
What does it take to figure all this out?

Why do you think that it's a ghost you meet?
Look at My wounds, and touch My hands and feet.

A ghost does not consist of flesh and bone."
Then more closely His hands and feet were shown.

Their faith in this did still with doubts compete,
And He asked, "Have you anything to eat?"

They gave Him fish, which Jesus took and ate.
"Peace be with you, and may you emulate.

Just as the Father sent Me, now do I send you."
And then, to give them help with all that would ensue,

He breathed on them, "Receive the Hold Spirit.
If you retain or pardon, God will hear it.

The ones you pardon will gain absolution,
While those with sins retained face retribution."

279 Jesus Appears to His Disciples (Thomas being Present)
Jn. 20:24-29

Now Thomas, an apostle called the Twin,
Had not been there when Jesus walked right in.

They told him, "Jesus stood before us, Thomas!"
Yet still he doubted that came true the promise.

 "I'll not believe. Until I see His hands and feet,
And feel His torn up flesh, my doubt will not deplete."

Then eight days hence, again in that same house they dwelt.
Christ entered, "Peace. Now, Thomas, what wounds need be felt?

Come place your finger in My hand, or in My side.
Do not lack faith. Believe I live, although I died."

In awe, Thomas cried, "My Lord and my God!"
"You thought this was a lie or a façade.

You only have this faith because you have seen Me.
Those who believe yet have not seen more blessed will be."

280 Christ Before the Eleven on a Mountain in Galilee
Mt. 28:16-20

Then the eleven went to Galilee,
Where they were told that Jesus they would see.

There, on the mountainside, Jesus appeared
And they prostrated and their Lord revered.

"On earth and heaven, all authority
The Father has seen fit to give to Me.

Preach to all nations that all people hear it.
In My name, and the Father and the Spirit,

Shall you baptize people from every land
And teach them to heed all things I command.

Baptized believers will receive salvation,
While people who reject face condemnation.

Those who believe will do many a sign,
For poison shall to them be like fresh wine.

Unharmed they'll pick up serpents and cast demons out,
And in strange tongues they do not know My words they'll shout.

They'll lay hands on the sick and they shall cure.
And I shall be with you forevermore."

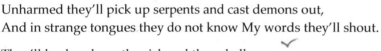

[394]

281 Jesus at the Sea of Tiberias
Jn. 21:1-23

Now one night Peter, the two sons of Zebedee,
Thomas, Nathanael from Cana in Galilee,

And two more followers together stood.
Said Peter, "I'll go fish. The skies look good."

They said to him, "We'll go with you as well."
Yet they caught not one fish to eat or sell.

When passed the night, stood Jesus at the shore,
Though who it was remained to them obscure.

He called, "My friends, have you not caught a thing?"
"We've not!" "Then starboard should you your nets swing!"

They did this and their nets became so full
They hardly could together their nets pull.

The follower Christ loved said, "It's the Lord!"
So Peter tied his garment with its cord

And in the water leaped. The rest got in the boat
And, since it could not hold them with the fish and float,

They dragged the net a hundred yards to shore.
When they reached land, they heard Jesus implore,

 "Come, eat with Me!" For He had fish and bread.
"Bring some fish you just caught here," Jesus said.

So Peter helped them pull the net out of the sea.
The fish therein numbered a hundred fifty-three.[233]

So they were shocked that their nets had not broken.
"Come and eat breakfast with Me," then was spoken.

To find out who He was no one implored,
For it was very clear it was the Lord.

Then Jesus handed them some fish and bread
And, after all of them were amply fed,

Asked, "Peter, do you love Me more than others?"
"You know I do." "Then feed My lambs like brothers."

Again He asked, "Peter, in truth, do you love Me?"
"I love You, Lord." "Then tend My sheep most faithfully."

A third time Christ asked, "Simon, do you love Me?"
So Peter said, "Your thoughts are leagues above me,

You know I love You," and this almost made him weep.
So Christ looked deeply into his eyes, "Feed My sheep."

Then Jesus said, "I tell you in all truth
You dressed and went where you willed in your youth.

Yet when you're old you shall stretch out your hands
And dress and walk as someone else demands."

Thus Jesus told them how would end his story,
How Peter's death would give God His due glory.

Then Christ said, "Follow Me. I'll be your guide.
I'm headed to the city where I died."[234]

When Peter saw the one Christ loved behind,
He asked, "Will his demise be as unkind?

Will he be killed as well when comes his turn?"
"Just follow Me. His end's not your concern."

The rumor then began that he would never die,
Yet only "It's not your concern," was His reply.

282 The Ascension
Lk. 24:44-53, Acts 1:6-11

Now Christ appeared to them for forty days
And taught them of the kingdom and its ways.

Once in Jerusalem, He sat with them again,
"I'd told you how I would be killed by evil men.

The Prophets, Law, and Psalms spoke this of Me,
And to fulfill them was My destiny."

He opened thus their minds to what the Scriptures said,
How "on the third day He would rise up from the dead,

That, in His name, repentance would be preached,
That sins be pardoned and all nations reached,

Spread from Jerusalem to the world's ends.
You shall give witness to all this, My friends.

The gift the Father promised I will not deny.
Stay here until you're clothed with power from on high.

For John baptized with water, being near the sea,
But baptized with the Holy Spirit you shall be."

Christ led to Bethany's outskirts, His plan unknown,
"Is your intention now to bring back David's throne?"

"It's not for you to know the time or season,
For God decides by His command and reason.

Yet from the Holy Spirit you'll gain power:
You'll spread My word worldwide when comes this hour."

Christ raised His hands, while blessing the eleven,
And He was raised, behind a cloud, to heaven.

They stood in awe, there, staring at the sky,
While, suddenly, two men in white stood by.

 "Why stare you skyward, men of Galilee?
What is up there that you intend to see?

This Jesus, who's been lifted and for whom you yearn,
Shall, in the same way as you saw Him leave, return."

They worshipped Christ and, going back elated,
Their praise was in the Temple elevated.

283 Pentecost
Acts 2:1-13

When Pentecost came, they were all assembled
And winds from heaven blew that the house trembled.

Then rested over them tongues as of fire,
To light them up and never to expire.

Then each of them was with the Holy Spirit filled
And spoke in foreign tongues just as the Spirit willed.

Nearby lived righteous men from every nation
Who came to hear this noise, this acclamation,

And, shockingly, they understood each word,
For in their native language it was heard.

They said, "In truth are Galileans here,
Yet my own tongue is what has reached my ear.

For we are Partheans, Arabs, and Elamites.
Asians, Medes, and Romans, both Jews and proselytes,

Judeans, Cappadocians, Pamphylians,
Mesopotamians, Libyans, Phrygians,

Men from Pontus, Egypt, Cyrene, and Crete!
And maybe more, should that be incomplete.

Somehow we hear it, each in our own tongue,
The marvels of our God, here loudly sung."

The people stood amazed at this event
And asked each other what they thought it meant.

A few, however, ridiculed this sign,
"These men have just been drinking too much wine."

284 Peter's address to the crowd
Acts 2:14-36

Then Peter stood with them and with a voice most loud,
Attested to the Spirit's work before the crowd,

"You men who live here, though you hail from far away,
Hear every word. Make no mistake on what I say.

We've had no drink, it being the third hour,
But acted as the Lord has given power.

For as the prophet foretold, 'In the final days,
I shall pour our My Spirit as the sun its rays,[235]

On all humanity, and this the Lord declares.
For your children a prophet's tongue shall then be theirs.

Your young men shall see visions while your old dream dreams.
Your male and female slaves shall also feel My beams,

[401]

And from them most prophetic words you'll know.
Great wonders in the heavens I will show

And signs on earth, signs greater than the flood.
The sun will turn to black, the moon to blood

When comes God's day, a day both terrible and great.
Who calls on God's name this day will see heaven's gate.'[236]

You men of Israel, hear what I say:
Jesus of Nazareth was sent our way
By God, with many wondrous works and signs,
That as you walk, a light among you shines.

You saw all this, how they delivered Him to die.
This was God's plan, and thus did prophets prophesy.

You had Him killed by men outside the law.
So God raised Him to life, from death's cold claw.

For Hades could not hold Him by its power,
As David drew him, 'I seek God each hour.

With Him at my right hand, I'll stand unshaken,
That I will not in Hades be forsaken,

Nor shall He let His own suffer corruption,
And so my heart rejoiced sans interruption,

My tongue delighted and I'll rest secure.
You taught me to the way of life procure.

With you I shall be filled with such elation.'[237]
We'll all agree, and with no hesitation,

That David's dead and buried, for his tomb is here.
But prophets know God's promises are most sincere

And God had sworn that one from his seed grown
Would be the one inheriting his throne.

He spoke not as a mirror gives reflection,
But of the Christ and of His resurrection.

He is the one from Hades swept away,
The one whose body suffered not decay.

God raised Him back to life, and all of this we saw.
Then He was lifted by the giver of the Law

To God's right hand, and having gained the Spirit,
Outpoured It here, that you now see and hear It.

Although in heaven David had not walked his feet,
He said, 'The Lord declared to my Lord, "Take your seat,

Prepared at My right hand, where you might rest with ease,
Till I make you a footstool from your enemies."'[238]

By all of Israel this shall not be denied,
This Lord God made is Jesus, whom you crucified."

285 The First Conversions
Acts 2:37-42

Now, hearing this, their hearts were cut right through,
And they asked Peter, "What are we to do?"

 "Repent of all the sins you've now realized
And in the name of Jesus be baptized.

Then, from your sinfulness you'll gain reprieve.
You, too, will the Holy Spirit receive!

God's promise is for you, your kids, those far away,
For He is calling all back to Himself today!"

He spoke much more, with great argumentation,
"Save yourselves from this sinful generation!"

They were baptized, accepting every word.
That very day three thousand joined their herd.

286 The Early Christian Community
Acts 2:43-47

They held true to the teachings and the brotherhood,
To breaking bread as kin, and praying for the good.

And the apostles left them filled with awe
When signs and miracles the faithful saw.

The brethren all sold everything that they possessed
And everything was doled out, more to those hard-pressed,

For all they owned they shared with all communally.
And with one heart they went to Temple constantly.

They met in houses for the breaking of the bread,
Where food was freely shared and praises to God said.

Then all admired how their company behaved
And daily did God add to those who would be saved.

The Appendix:
Jesus Descends to the Dead[1]
Mt. 27:51-53, 1 Peter 3:18-19

Then Christ descended into Hades, where there dwelt
Those who had died, who neither pain nor pleasure felt,

Save what they had brought with them at the start,
If joy or misery sprung from their heart.

This place had never seen the light of day
And all things there were in a shade of gray.

At first, just as an endless mass did they appear,
But Christ saw all them differently as they drew near,

Not as just grains of sand that never reach the shores.
As great as were their sins in life were now their sores.

Some almost looked as people would on earth,
While some seemed that they monsters were from birth,

So utterly grotesque did they appear.
From this they now could hardly see or hear.

On seeing Christ, all drenched in blood, the devil said,
"I offered You the world and You chose death instead!

You taught about Your realm, Your fantasy!
See what befalls who will not worship me!

For all Your words of charity and love,
What help was sent by Your Father above?!

1

This is the one passage in the entire book which is not based on the Gospels. It is almost entirely based on my own imagination and theological reflection. In the Apostle's Creed, Christians profess that Jesus "descended to the dead," which is based on 1 Peter 3:18-19 This passage also mentions that Jesus preached to those "in prison" during the time, which means those who had died must have still had the opportunity to accept or reject Jesus' message. (I would entirely reject the idea that the unbaptized were all doomed to hell, as could be found in the Divine Comedy, since this would make God incredibly cruel, far more than even his cruelest creatures.) In this appendix, I imagined what a scene in which Jesus preached to the dead may possibly have been like. I am not in any way claiming that divine inspiration led me to write this. I merely thought this, like any sermon or parable, was something people could meditate on, learn a lesson from, or be inspired by.

You tried to teach to mankind agape.
I taught them how to kill their God today!

You thought their sins abhorrent were before?!
They'll only grow more evil evermore!

You dared cast out my demons with such power,
But for the victory this is my hour."

"I did not come here for to waste My breath
On one who reeks of hatred, lies, and death.

For I have passed through all this blood and strife
To teach to the deceased the way of life."

"Yours is the way of life? You must be joking!
That's like if a physician prescribed choking!

You said You gave Your life up for your friends.
Yet at Your trial none of them defends.

One worked for me, but where were the eleven?
You who could have armies descend from heaven

Instead nonviolently obey Your Lord.
My men have conquered earth with spear and sword!

You have received Your brutal death today
For following Your stupid selfless way!"

"You hung yourself and now are tightening the rope.
I did not come to waste time on those beyond hope,"

Christ said to Satan and addressed the crowd.
Despite its size, His voice was amply loud.

"All you deceased your God did not forget.
Your guilt will cease when evil you regret.

You've worshipped many gods, but there is only one.
I have been sent to sanctify you, as His Son.

For many of you lived lives of adultery,
Theft, malice, murder, rape, fraud, and dishonesty,

Greed, jealousy, and insubordination,
Drunken debauchery and fornication,

Lives lived as if the greatest goal was pleasure,
As if the greater man had greater treasure,

Such pride you loved yourselves and not another,
Just walking past when met with starving brother.

These former ways must feel your hatred and contempt.
You must not let him into further darkness tempt.

You've lived with sin and guilt and know it is no friend.
Receive My blood and all your tortured guilt will end!

Receive My agape and shed your malice."
And, while imploring them, Christ showed His chalice.

Then Satan scoffed, "I, too, could end their pain.
Regretting sinful ways is just insane.

Though You may criticize our selfishness and hate,
You don't say they who live Your way receive Your fate.

You lost our duel! We nailed You to the cross!
And no one here would want to share Your loss!

We here would have to be as dumb as mud
To listen to a man immersed in blood.

[408]

I only wish that I could have those men
Right here to nail Your hands and feet again!

I wish that I could use the whip from which You bled
And drive myself the crown of thorns into Your head!"

A man came who for years had never smiled,
Built like a soldier, weeping like a child,

 "I have been dwelling in this place for years
And can see nothing through my sores and tears.

For those I should have loved most in my life,
My five boys, three girls, and my darling wife,

I should have loved so much I'd give my life to save!
Instead, I harshly beat them dare they misbehave.

If ever just my violent urge was felt,
Unto the nearest one a blow was dealt.

And when I had been drinking too much wine,
I even could take turns beating all nine.

Not one attack have I been able to forget.
I spend each day in this damned place filled with regret.

I searched for them for years throughout the land
And why I've found them not I understand.

I've scoured all through this land again and again,
A hundred times more leagues than Alexander's men.

They hide regardless of how hard I search down here!
In life, regrets I told them of were not sincere.

I gladly would tread a nonviolent course
To end my isolation and remorse.

For Socrates knew what men must not contradict:
'It better is to suffer hardship than inflict.'

I choose Your way and from it will not swerve,
Not even should I feel all I deserve."

Now clearly all this man said he believed
So humbly he the blood of Christ received.

As Christ received the man with such great joy,
There walked in their direction a young boy,

Just eight years old, for long on earth he did not live.
Yet he was first of all the man's kin to forgive.

In time, his wife came, and the other seven
And they felt they already were in heaven.

A woman came to Jesus then and said,
"I did not give myself when I was wed.

When things were tough and difficult the day,
My husband worked while I would sneak away.

I went and laid with someone else's man,
While fully knowing this against God's plan.

It was not even one mistake I made,
But many times with someone else I laid.

And, as I was not to my husband true,
I never told him though I'm sure he knew.

For after I another man would hold
To my own husband I was icy cold.

In here, just as in life, my husband lies with me,
But it is like he's in a stranger's company.

I gave my darling such pain for my pleasure,
Which only dealt us both grief beyond measure.

I don't deserve Your mercy, or that of my spouse!
I broke Your most just law and brought shame to his house.

What once gave pleasure now gives me disgust.
I never was in life deserving trust,

But now I know my guilt and for forgiveness pray
And know that living for myself is not the way."

Christ then embraced her, followed by her husband true.
"Would that your former lover felt the same as you,"

Hoped Jesus, and this man did soon appear,
Who, though requested, walked there filled with fear.

 "I see that You forgive adultery,
But also murder and hypocrisy?!

As well as often cheating on my wife,
Whom I should have been true to all my life,

I ruined marriages that were not mine.
I only cared for women, food, and wine.

Once, while I was walking through the town square,
A crowd came dragging someone by her hair,

All screaming, "Sinner!" "Whore!" "Adultery!"
And as the mob passed, they were joined by me.

[411]

Though they were mad, and following the Law,
I had the power to the mob declaw.

Had I protested, it was possible,
Yet all I thought was she was beautiful

And wished that I, instead, had been her lover,
But wanted all to think I was above her,

Not allied with her, like I shared her station.
I only cared to save my reputation.

Not only did I let her die, I threw a stone,
That from her piercing scream I knew it shattered bone.

I should have fought to teach the crowd compassion,
But I knew throwing stones was more in fashion.

Now I am begging You show mercy and forgive,
Though I would not do such to help a person live."

 "I even can forgive such cruel hypocrisy
And those who swear allegiance to mobocracy,

So long as you your sinful ways regret
And have your heart towards selfless ends reset."

 "I want Your way of love, where all is sacrificed,"
The man insisted and was welcomed in by Christ.

[412]

Then two came, "Were this all a competition,
We two would have the most need of contrition."

 "It's not from sores, but shame we hide our faces,
For we are two of mankind's worst disgraces!

For, though we worked hard, we were very poor.
When crops grew well, our landlord just took more."

 "No one would give us help, nor even lend.
It seemed as if the hunger would not end.

Each night with stomachs aching would we go to sleep
Till we decided we would not our baby keep.

We left her sleeping in the wilderness!
We merit nothing but this dark abyss,

To have no happiness in endless time,
To spend it all regretting our great crime!

For, as we lived our lives ourselves to serve,
If anything more hurt do we deserve."

 "Even if we should bleed as much as You,
Then justice would be all that we went through.

We can't undo our sinful choice that day,
But now will we accept Your selfless way."

They drank and, physically, the same were feeling
And, like the rest, their guilt began its healing.

On seeing their remorse, then came to them
A man who wanted to himself condemn.

"In life, I took more than they could afford.
I was their greedy, heartless, cruel landlord.

For more valued than any block of silver
Was land that bordered on the Yangtze River.

I loved my money more than wife or son,
Like he who died with the most treasure won.

I did not work, nor read great books, nor pray,
And rather than with my young children play,

I would spend hours counting all my cash,
Delighting how had multiplied the stash.

I'd fantasize how it could all increase,
How pockets full could make me look obese.

I dreamed how at all worse off I could scoff
And get my will by buying someone off.

Like I was God, I'd get all I desire!
There was no end to where I could aspire.

And there was nothing I would not do for this end:
Fierce threats or violence, theft or hurting my best friend.

As for their girl, in truth, I did not know,
Nor did I have the mercy to bestow.

For had I cared to know their daughter's life was spent,
I would use that excuse that they could pay more rent.

By being with my treasures so obsessed,
I was by everything I owned possessed.

We feasted while our tenants had an empty bowl,
But they had nothing half as empty as my soul.

I was so shocked to come down here to see
The wretched poor much happier than me.

For they are here with family and friends
While I, for all my life and selfish ends,

Do not have in my pocket one denarri.
And only seeing this did I feel sorry.

As I have naught with which to pay them off,
In my direction did they laugh and scoff.

Just now I see how others were affected.
I see my sins, which cannot be corrected.

Though I looked great in life, in my own eyes,
All I once loved in life I now despise.

Though, in life, Satan, I followed your way.
I hate it now and spit on you today!"

And spit he did, to Satan's great surprise,
Aimed perfectly into the demon's eyes.
"You fool!" screamed Satan, filled with rage and hate,
"You like His way? You want to share His fate?!

Much better did you know, or so I thought,
For you had learned so well all that I taught.

Though I should treat you as you treated me,

[415]

And let you suffer through eternity,

Thanks to your years of service you won't have my hate,
But I will warn instead that you shall share His fate."

"Do you not know?! Because I sinned their daughter died!
Bring here the cross and nails that I be crucified!!

When I bleed, all here will hear me rejoice,
That I for once have made a noble choice!

Choke on your egocentric way of life!
And, if I must, I will endure the knife."

Just then, before his Lord, he humbly knelt
And by Satan was such betrayal felt.

"How can You pardon me, who did his bidding?
One can't shake Satan's hand and say they're kidding."

"So have it your way," Satan then replied,
"And bow down to the God I crucified.

For my revenge, I won't one finger raise,
But use one who was faithful all these days.

I'll have you tortured by a master of the trade,
Who at the urge, would his helpless neighbors invade.

For facing him, I do not envy you.
No evil deed in life would he not do.

Go torture him! Go do your master's will!"
Yet this man said, "I will not serve you still.

I led men to many a town and village,
To plunder, burn, to murder, rape, and pillage.

I raised their bloodlust to a heartless rage
To murder innocents of every age.

We caused such suffering, as was our pleasure,
And I made sure that I controlled the treasure.

The streets ran red, for my men did as told,
For I took all they had to have their gold.

The children's faces, I can see them all,
Still in their mothers' arms and still so small.

Their terrified expressions thrilled my men,
Who, if they could, would slaughter them again.

For all their inhumane dastardly things,
I was the puppet master pulling strings.

They begged for mercy and, as if a game,
We left them raped as widows they became.

We had the power over life or death,
To spare a life or take away one's breath.

As much as each of my men fought to get their gold,
This power is just too much for men to behold.

Once we discovered iron weaponry,
No decent opposition did we see.

In sole possession of this deadly power,
We needed just to choose the place and hour.

Then often, as they slept, our hammer fell,
Converting peaceful dreaming into hell,

Invading homes to cruelly end their lives,
While helplessly those men laid with their wives.

We made a sport of bringing their demise,
Of seeing fear and tears filling their eyes.

When they, so desperate, for our mercy pled,
We laughed at them and slit their throats instead.

No true mercy to them was ever shown,
As if the concept was not by us known.

Our reputation gave people such fear
That when the rumor spread my men drew near,

They'd offer tribute, that we'd stay away,
And every coin they could afford they'd pay.

So when I lacked the vigor of my youth,
I used this fear to add more gold, in truth,

For no longer was bloodshed my intention,
But not one word of this could I e'er mention.

Then, as I made my rounds, and people paid,
I saw who I widows and orphans made,

The children who were merely skin and bone,
The mothers crying as the children groan.

Then did I realize all that I had done,
How battles can be lost, but never won,

How much it hurts to see a child cry,
How hard to look the mother in the eye.

In one moment, my hate turned to compassion,
But for a soldier, mercy's not in fashion.

From guilt, I'd cry when darkness hid the day,
But still would I make rounds to get my pay.

Though I knew how abhorrent was my crime,
I still did not return to them one dime.

I should have taken that as inspiration,
To give them back some sort of reparation.

For what good is compassion or regret
If it is not with matching actions met?

A change of heart is grossly incomplete
If it can move your tears but not your feet.

I should have given to them all my wealth,
But I was too much in love with myself.

Had I these treasures here with me today,
I'd, in an instant, give it all away.

And now when, Satan, I look in your eyes,
I see my former way, which I despise.

I see your way, of hatred and disdain,
Of reveling in other people's pain.

Your former general makes this declaration,
With joy, that now I know emancipation,

I'll never do for you another thing!
I vow allegiance to this newfound king!

If he should judge that torture I deserve,
I'll bear it all and then I'll gladly serve,"

He knelt, "If you will have me, I will serve you, Lord."
"There's no end to the mercy which I can afford,

When with sincere regret mercy is sought.
I urge, regardless what in life you thought,

You all accept the Most High God, the only one,
And that I am His messenger and only Son.

If you abandon sinful ways today,
I'll pardon all and you may walk My way."

"You come down here with us, all crucified,
Imploring that the way You walked be tried.

If those who followed me should Your way choose,
I do not care, for nothing will I lose.

I was not one to heed Your Father's will.
I had my pride and have maintained it still.

For Your way, You've already Your life lost.
If I need beg them, it's not worth the cost.

I thought more of them when I was their guide,
For now they have surrendered all their pride.

Kneel down, you fools, if you want this man as your Christ!
I won't, for nothing could be worth what's sacrificed."

Then millions came, from every race and nation,
Who sought and found their reconciliation.

Some had great sins, as those folks you heard of,
And turned their hearts from selfishness to love.

In truth, the sins of many were so slight
The rest marveled that they were so contrite,

For every minor sin and indiscretion
And even accidents were their confession.

For them, Christ needed not from evil ways persuade,
But merely urge them that the leap of faith be made.

Yet those there numbered like the stars in all the sky,
And many did not likewise to His pleas reply.

Great crowds stood still, or laughed in their direction,
And some said why they would not take correction.

 "I will not take heartache wrapped up in virtue,"
Said one man, "We see how Your path has hurt You.

And I see no need ever to repent.
For, as I am right now, I am content.

I can't say I regret one single pleasure,
While You've been made to suffer beyond measure.

To suffer for another, like I've been enslaved!
From that foolish position I would need be saved.

I'd only suffer were it for my gain.
To do anything else would be insane."

Christ said, "I pity you, so empty is your heart.
I have shown you the way to virtue, for My part."

"Virtue is for the poor," another said,
"Those who need beg their neighbors for their bread,

When kindness only can improve one's station.
For me, I used threats and manipulation,

And could they still my own happiness bring,
I'd do to those around me anything.

Had I the inkling to apologize,
I'd only need to see Your blood-soaked eyes

To know how useless is a life of virtue,
To stand there peacefully while others hurt you!

[422]

Should You be God, that still won't be my way.
That's why I'm staying where I stand today."

Great crowds then cheered him, as they shared his sentiment,
Finding no reason to their sinful ways repent.

Then, finally was Jesus brought to tears,
"I'd plead with you here for a million years

If I thought it would change one single mind,
But I can't heal those happy to be blind.

From sin's true fruits you've thus far been protected.
But if your final chance is now rejected,

If this last opportunity's not taken,
You shall be by your evil overtaken!

If you do not reject your sin in whole,
It will consume you all, body and soul!

If you do not believe Me and beseech My aid,
It shall become the last mistake you ever made.

Please come to Me and kill your sin today.
Then, in your goodness, you can walk My way."

Crowds moved, each like a tree which cut off its own root,
While still so many stayed, insanely resolute.

Then when the last one had received the blood of Christ,
Those who chose virtue felt as if their sores were sliced.

What were their sores were covered now in blood
And anguish overtook them like a flood,

While those who were with Satan still allied
Were more convinced they chose the better side,

For what had given them such pain before
Did not one bit of hurt give anymore.

The sight of them could still make one recoil:
What had been sores had transformed into oil.

Since they no longer felt an ounce of pain,
They laughed, rejoicing at their latest gain.

Then Satan asked, "Are you shocked to be thus adorned?!
You can't complain to me that you had not been warned!

You had the chance and His way was your choice,
So seeing you in pain will I rejoice!

Now shall you witness how great is my power,
How stupid you were, for this is my hour!"

 "So says the biggest fool of all time," Christ replied,
"They are not being punished, but are purified."

Christ raised His arms up and His blood just disappeared,
His bruises left and, as one whom need be revered,

His whole appearance changed before their sight,
His flesh and even robe shone forth such light

That it was like they all were staring at the sun,
Without the pain, a light that could not be outdone.

 "At least they knew to heed what was revealed.
Now they are fine." And just then they were healed.

The blood on them quickly evaporated,
Which left them indescribably elated.

Christ told the devil, "God had treated you like kin,
While, stubbornly, you've stood here glorifying sin.

You've spewed forth hatred, avarice, and guile,
Pride, anger, vengeance, and all that is vile.
To cause torment is your greatest desire.
So now shall you endure unending fire!"

On hearing this, the devil was engulfed in flame.
He shrieked in agony and cursed Jesus' name.

To all around him quickly was the fire spread,
Who begged it to consume them and just leave them dead.

They screamed at Jesus, cursed Him and they loudly swore,
But their hope would abandoned be forevermore.

Then Jesus said to those people who chose His way,
"You are the children of the Most High God today!

You followed Me regardless what that meant,
So you shall know unending merriment,

Elation never felt in all the earth,
Not at a wedding or a child's birth.

For thus far has your view of joy been shallow:
Compared to heaven, earth is but a shadow.

Till now, you have not known true ecstasy,
Nor the extent one can feel joie de vie.

Rejoice, my friends, with heartfelt exultation,
That you shall live in such endless elation!

Part of your maker's family you have become,
So let yourself with happiness be overcome!

We should not waste more time in this dark place,
While you still wait to see your Father's face.

Come with Me, friends, to joy unseen before,
Where we shall laugh and sing forevermore."

[1] This reference to Psalms 23: 5 is an addition.

[2] This foreshadowing of Zechariah's being made mute is an addition.

[3] Zechariah, to whom this passage was addressed, was from the priestly class of Abijah, meaning he was a distant descendant of Abijah. It also happens to be one of the only things that rhymes with Elijah.

[4] Palatine was considered the most important of the Seven Hills of Rome.

[5] For a woman to be childless was one of the greatest shames a woman could endure in 1st century Palestine.

[6] The Gospel does not, of course, make any reference to Mary's beauty. However, when my grandfather was suffering with Parkinson's disease, Jesus and Mary appeared to him, telling him they were with him through his suffering. He described Mary as the most beautiful woman he had ever seen, which is my basis for including that.

[7] The angel Gabriel appears in the book of Daniel, making a messianic prediction

[8] Several Bibles and commentaries, whether they translated it to say the power of God would "overshadow" Mary, or "cover you with its shadow," or some similar variation thereof, agreed that this was an allusion to the cloud that covered Mt. Sinai, when Moses received the Commandments, and/or the cloud that guided the people through the Sinai desert.

[9] Agape (αγαπη) is the Greek word for self-sacrificing Christian love. Due to the poverty of the English language, we use the same word for "I love my wife," and "I love mint chocolate chip ice cream." We have no word for agape. We also have no word for joi de vie, an absence which may be related.

[10] Her exact greeting of "Shalom" is my own addition.

[11] In keeping with the theme of the text, I added the innocent being freed from prison, based on biblical figures such as John the Baptist, Peter, and Paul, and modern ones, such as Gandhi, Martin Luther King Jr., Phil and Dan Berrigan, John Dear, and Kathy Kelly.

[12] "The Lord is gracious" is the meaning of the name John.
Although the gathered community did not want this name,
they would certainly have agreed with the sentiment.

[13] This is, of course, an addition.

[14] Elizabeth first prophesied about her son and, now, Zechariah does the same. (For poetic reasons, 4-syllable names often have to be replaced with pronouns.)

[15] This is one place where I take the liberty of openly disagreeing with the Gospel writer. Luke, likely for dramatic purposes, has Mary leave Elizabeth before the birth of John the Baptist, in order to finish the story of Mary's visit before telling the story of John's birth. The problem is, if she really spent three months helping out her elderly, pregnant cousin, and left right before she went into labor, Mary would be about as stupid and insensitive as your average sitcom husband.

[16] Although a betrothed coupled did not yet live together, or have sexual relations, cheating on your betrothed by fornicating with someone else was punishable by death

[17] These several lines explaining the law and imagining what Joseph was going through are an addition. For those who wonder why Joseph does not forgive Mary's supposed infidelity, it was against Mosaic law to raise a child as your own if you were not the biological father.

[18] At this time, a person would refer to their betrothed as their husband or wife. The final stage of engagement in this culture was the man taking the woman into his house and them consummating the marriage.

[19] Jesus means "Yahweh saves."

[20] Isaiah 7:14. The original text refers to a young woman, not specifying whether or not she was a virgin, but the Greek translation of the Old Testament, the Septuagint, had translated this passage as "virgin" long before Matthew was written.

[21] The final stage of engagement.

[22] I avoided the reference to Quirinius being governor of Syria because of its likely historical inaccuracy, and because it bears so little importance on the story. My main reason was not that Quirinius, like 99% of Biblical names, rhymes with almost nothing.

[23] While this is not in the text, the Romans took about 50% of what Israelites earned, leaving many malnourished. This would have, definitely, been the purpose of a census.

[24] Lánúin is Gaelic for a married couple.

[25] The passage is quoted by the wise men, in Matthew, while the surrounding material here is Lukan. I think all scholars would agree that Luke was appealing to the same Old Testament text, Micah 5:2.

[26] Reference to John 16:21

[27] Luke's Gospel makes 3 mentions of Mary and Joseph following Jewish law in this passage. As commentators have pointed out, Mary needed to be purified while Jesus needed to be consecrated to God and redeemed. This did not have to be done at the Temple, but doing so was not incredibly unlikely, since Jerusalem was only about 5 miles away from Bethlehem. According to Luke, Jesus' parents went to Jerusalem every year and John has Jesus go there at least 3 times during his public ministry.

[28] Ex. 13:2,12

[29] Luke only mentions that Mary and Joseph followed the law that required the sacrifice of either turtledoves or pigeons. I used turtledoves because it rhymed and because of "The Twelve Days of Christmas."

[30] Micah 5:2

[31] Hosea 11:1

[32] Jer. 31: 15

[33] The most likely Old Testament reference scholars have pointed to for this prediction of the Messiah is Judges 13:5,7 ("the boy will be a Nazirite"), which does not seem very Messianic. Since we do not know what copy, if any, of the Old Testament Matthew had, or if he was even quoting from memory, I stick to my policy of not correcting a quote unless we can be absolutely certain of its error.

[34] As I mentioned before, agape (Greek for unselfish love) and joie de vie (French for an exhilaration from enjoying life) are words that lack English equivalents. I think that people who exhibit agape, while it may involve picking up one's cross, will experience joie de vie unlike anything a selfish person can ever experience.

[35] While I do use a bit of imagination to describe a playful Jesus, he uses these three verbs in Mt. 11:17, in one of His descriptions of children.

[36] The text does not say how he grew in wisdom. Although observation and experience are other sources of obtaining wisdom, suffering is certainly one of the main ways humans become wise.

[37] In Biblical times, it was, of course, forbidden to speak the name of God, Yahweh. This is because, in Semitic culture, to say someone's name means that you have power over them, and no one could ever have any power over God. In our culture, however, to say someone's name merely means that the person has revealed to us his/her identity. Given this set of values, it would be dishonest not to use the name of God sometimes.

[38] The city of David is, of course, Jerusalem.

[39] Isaiah 40:3.

[40] "Healing baths" refers to John's baptism which brought a spiritual healing, rather than the conventional Roman meaning of a "healing bath".

[41] The symbolism of a baptism is that a person symbolically dies (through drowning) and, coming out of the water, is born anew. While perfection is not expected, the goal is that one's sinful ways die and the person tries to lead a life free of sin, to the best of his/her ability. This explanation is not in the original text.

[42] While John is demanding good works be shown as a sign of repentance, the saying that faith without good works is dead comes from James 2:17.

[43] Jesus being baptized was considered problematic, since Christians have always held that He was sinless and the purpose of baptism, at least for everyone else, was the forgiveness of sins and a change of heart. Although John does not perform the baptism in the John's Gospel, I went with the Synoptic tradition, in which Jesus was baptized, although His had a different purpose.

[44] Dt. 8:3.

[45] Psalms 91:11,12.

[46] Dt. 6:16.

[47] I added Satan's claim that he has driven the ways of the world, although the claim that he owns the world and that it was given to him are both from the Gospel accounts.

[48] Dt. 6:13.

[49] This metaphor is an addition.

[50] It is generally thought that Nicodemus meets Jesus at night because he is too scared to be seen with Him during the day. He will, however, become more courageous, giving Jesus a half-defense when they want to kill him, saying the law demands a trial, and then burying Jesus, when this would have been incredibly risky.

[51] Nicodemus is confused in this passage because Jesus' words could either mean "born again" or "born from above." I translated Jesus' saying to be "born anew" because this is what Nicodemus hears, even though it was not Jesus' meaning. Otherwise, his response seems bizarre.

[52] This statement is an addition.

[53] This reference to Jesus as God's Word is an addition, borrowed from John's Prologue.

[54] Samaria is located in between Galilee and Judea. Following the Assyrian exile (722 BC), those who lived in Samaria intermarried with people sent from the east by Assyria. After the Babylonian exile (586 BC) and their return (539 BC), Samaritans offered to help the Judeans rebuild the Temple that David and Solomon built and the Babylonians destroyed. When this offer was rejected, Samaritans built their own temple at Mount Gerizim. In addition to the difference of where worship was to take place, Samaritans only recognized the five books of Torah as being divinely inspired Scripture, while Jews believed in the writings of the Prophets and other books which make up their Bible.

[55] "Living water" could refer to water that flows naturally as opposed to water from a well. Jesus meant water that gives life.

[56] Isaiah 61:1-2.

[57] These two stories of Elijah and Elisha can be found in 1 Kings 17:7-24 and 2 Kings 5:1-19.

[58] I added this line as a brief explanation as to how Christ was able to merely "pass through their midst."

[59] Isaiah 53:4.

[60] The same apostle is known as Matthew in Matthew's Gospel and Levi in Mark and Luke's Gospels.

[61] This metaphor is an addition.

[62] Tax collectors and those who associated with them were so despised because they collected money for Israel's pagan oppressors (taxes which were about half of a person's income) and often collected extra to keep for themselves.

[63] Hosea 6:6

[64] When the wine fermented, it would need room to expand. Old wineskins had already been stretched, so new wineskins were needed for new wine. In Jesus' comparison, the old wineskins represent those elements of Judaism which He intends to replace.

[65] Hosea 6:6.

[66] Isaiah 42:1-4.

[67] Much of the material in Matthew's Sermon on the Mount can also be found in Luke's Sermon on the Plain. Rather than divide them into two speeches and randomly place the shared material in one sermon or the other, I combined them and, since Matthew's speech is much larger and better known, I used his setting. The one exception to this is the Beatitudes. Matthew has a list of Beatitudes ("Blessed are the poor in spirit…"), while Luke has a list of blessings ("Blessed are the poor…") and woes ("Woe to you rich…"). Since these could not easily be combined or placed side by side, I moved Luke's blessings and woes to right after the story of the rich man and Lazarus.

[68] An added reference to Jn. 16:21.

[69] Although salt cannot literally lose its flavor, it can become spoiled in a way that one would not want to use it.

[70] This image of seeds is not in the text, but it is certainly consistent with the light image and parables such as the parable of the sower.

[71] Again, this simile is not from the Gospel, but seemed appropriate.

[72] In this passage, as well as in the passage of anger, I do not think the mere feeling is what is condemned, since these feelings are instinctual and psychologically unhealthy to avoid entirely. I think Christ's first point is to avoid things that lead to sin. If you do not harbor anger and resentment, you will not kill. If you do not dwell on feelings of lust, you will not commit adultery. Also, if you do not commit adultery (or murder) because of a lack of opportunity (she doesn't find you attractive/isn't willing to sin with you) or fear (your wife would castrate you if she found out), but still desperately want to, you bear the same amount of guilt as someone who has the opportunity and willingness and actually does the crime.

[73] I thought this would be a nice way to take the traditional blame off the woman who, by her mere appearance, causes a man to feel temptation.

[74] Specifically, guilty of committing "adultery in your heart."

[75] Gehenna was an ancient garbage dump. It had formerly been the site where people (Jews and gentiles) sacrificed babies to Moloch/Molech, the god of pleasure. When the Israelites returned from their exile, they were so disgusted at what had been done there that they made it a place where a perpetual flame was, to burn their garbage. Jesus used this place of evil, heat and terrible stench as His image of hell.

[76] The exact translation of this word, "porneia", has been debated for centuries. Since there is no exception for divorce in the other Gospels, Catholics have viewed this as a solution for marriages that pagans may have partaken in before converting to Christianity, which would have been against Mosaic law (i.e. incestuous marriages). Hence, only a pre-existing condition can make a marriage contract invalid under Catholic canon law. Many Protestant and Orthodox churches, however, translate "porneia" to mean a breach in the law of marriage, namely adultery. Therefore, they allow people to obtain a divorce if their spouse commits adultery.

[77] The text actually says the altar (part of the Temple) and Jerusalem, the city of the great king (and home of the Temple).

[78] The best explanation for the "turn the other cheek" passage is that Jesus is not telling us to, like someone being hazed, to say, "Please, sir, I'd like another." Slapping was done as an insult, with the back of one hand, to say someone was inferior to yourself (A husband would strike his wife, a parent would strike their child, a master would strike a slave, etc.). If you, therefore, turned your cheek, the person would be forced to either not strike you or declare you an equal.

[79] Again, in Jewish culture, people would wear only two things, an undergarment and an outer garment. And, in terms of shame, when a person was seen naked, the shame was felt by the person seeing the naked person, not by the person who was themselves nude. Jesus is saying that if someone steals or sues you for your outer garment to give him shame by giving the undergarment as well.

[80] The part about us lacking God's wisdom and vision is my own addition. The following 8 lines are based, not on the Gospels, but on Romans 12: 17-21.
Many people treat Paul's letters as if the thoughts were entirely his own and the "Pauline" letters as if those thoughts likely also came from Paul, by means of a writer who learned Christianity from Paul. It is just as likely that Paul got his thoughts from his teacher, and that these thoughts were accurately passed down from Jesus. Reading Romans 12, it sounds as much like a sermon of Christ's as it does Pauline advice.

[81] There may seem to be a contradiction between this passage (as well as the following passages on prayer and fasting) and the urge to be a light to all people. The solution is simple, that if you only do good when people are watching, for the sheer sake of an improved reputation, then there is no reward to be granted by God. Yet if you always live a virtuous life, people will see this and imitate it.

[82] Christ is not against public prayer ("Whenever two or three gather…"), but against public displays of private individual prayer.

[83] This line is not from the Sermon on the Mount, but certainly has parallels in the Gospels and other New Testament writings, esp. James 5:1-6.

[84] This part about buying things for one's wife I added, but is certainly a motivation today for people becoming wealthy.

[85] Solomon was famous, not only for his wisdom, but for his incredible amount of silver, gold, etc.

[86] "Tomorning" is a Middle English word combining "tomorrow" and "morning."

[87] The last two lines are Luke's ending of this passage, while the two before it are Matthew's ending to it.

[88] Some people make the mistake of taking this to the logical extreme, thinking that if they forgive everyone, even if the person does not regret or repent of their sins, theirs will be forgiven by God, without repentance or regret. These two things were understood to be necessary preconditions for forgiveness by everyone until recent times.

[89] Jesus does not say that the road to destruction is downhill, but merely that it is easy. Obviously, up is often symbolic of God, goodness, heaven, etc. and down of moral decline, hell and the devil. And what makes a road more easy or difficult to walk than being uphill or downhill?

[90] This couplet is added, but in the spirit of the preceding lines. It comes from a condensed retelling of Chaucer's "The Pardoner's Tale", which I wrote years ago.

[91] A reference I added from the parable of the sower.

[92] Yes, fellow Christians, we worship a homeless guy!

[93] This man is not saying that he must bury a father who has just recently died but, rather, wait for his elderly father to pass away and then bury him.

[94] Mal. 3:1.

[95] According to II Kings 2:11, "Elijah went up by a whirlwind into heaven." (RSV)

[431]

[96] The likeness to pigs, an unclean animal, is an addition.

[97] These four lines (beginning with "Let anyone…") are my translation of the line that appears several times in the Synoptic Gospels, "He who has ears, let him hear." The Greek word used in the texts for "hear", "ακουω", also can mean "learn", "obey", and "understand". I feel certain that Christ, in using this play on words, was not singling out those with the physical ability to hear, but saying that those who can hear His words should learn them, understand them, and obey them.

[98] Jesus' explanation to the reason He speaks in parables is one of the more difficult passages in the New Testament. He says that "For whoever has, to him more shall be given, and he will have an abundance; but whoever does not have, even what he has shall be taken away from him." (Mt. 13:12) This seems a complete reversal of "He has filled the hungry with good things; and sent away the rich empty-handed." (Lk. 1:53) Raymond Brown conclusively showed that this text in Matthew referred to the Old Testament. Those who understood the central messages of it (agape, justice, faithfulness to God, etc.) would receive greater understanding, while those who did not understand the Old Testament, lowering it to a legalistic faith, or using it for power, would have even greater confusion than before.

[99] The image of a road and people thinking they gain God's promised inheritance by merely knowing how to walk is an addition.

[100] "Pelf" is a Middle English word for wealth, most especially ill-begotten wealth. (Many great theologians have made the case that virtually all wealth is ill-begotten, an argument that is virtually air-tight.)

[101] Since the man who scatters seed does not know how they grow, and "the very hairs of your head are all numbered" (Mt. 10:30), many have interpreted the man to be a prophet, any person who spreads the word.

[102] The original parable does not have this shepherd metaphor, but I think it common enough to be used freely. In the Gospels, tending sheep is described as a job of the Father, the Son, and good Christians in general.

[103] The text does not actually say that the enemy is consumed by hate and greed, but merely that he (or she?) is an enemy. Were this a real story, greed is the only other logical motivation to destroy another's crops (lowering the supply to increase the demand).

[104] This simile is an addition.

[105] The text actually says the just will shine like the sun, not "like stars".

[106] Since Christ uses the phrase "He who has ears, let him hear," to conclude many teachings, I repeat my four-line interpretation of this as a kind of refrain at the end of these teachings.

[107] The original does not give any indication as to what time of day this event occurred. However, it is almost universal in human societies to link the sun's rising with birth and its setting with death.

[108] "Legion" had one and only one meaning: a group of 5,000-6,000 Roman soldiers. Given that this story takes place in pagan territory, in a cemetery (both symbolic of death and ritually unclean), the demons enter a herd of swine (very un-kosher) who then head to the sea (where the Romans came from), the implications against imperialism and militarism should be noted.

[109] I found it a shame that we did not know this girl's name, and that she is only known throughout the three Gospels that tell her story as "the girl" or "the child." Since Jesus said to her, "Little girl, I say to you, arise," (RSV) I gave her the name Colleen, which is merely an Irish name that means "little girl."

[110] Scholars have debated as to which feast this was, some suggesting Tabernacles, Passover, Pentecost, Purim, or Rosh Hashanah. What can be said for certain is it was believed that, at this feast, after the water was disturbed, the first person to jump into the water would be healed of their ailments.

[111] Different ancient texts refer to this place as Bethzatha, Bethsaida, or Bethesda. I merely chose Bethesda because it rhymes.

[112] John's Gospel says that the Son, and in other places the Father, judges who gets into heaven. If you look at the Synoptics, both Peter and all 12 apostles are named as the people who judge.

[113] Matthew and Mark both show Herod believing Jesus to be John the Baptist raised from the dead, while Luke has him say that it could not be John because Herod had him beheaded.

[114] The original King Herod had ten wives and many of his sons and grandsons were known as "Herod", which has caused considerable confusion. Scholars believe that Herod married his half-brother's wife, dismissing his own wife for another married woman. Herodias was first married to a different Herod, while Philip was the husband of Salome, Herodias' daughter. The sin John was condemning could have been incest, adultery, or both.

[115] These similes, metaphors, etc. involving Jesus being a bread that can rise without leaven, wine and wheat, a lifeless desert, and the ship are my own additions.

[116] Carpe panem!" is another addition, which is Latin for "Seize the bread!"

[117] Ex. 20:12/Dt. 5:16

[118] Ex. 21:17/Lev. 20:9

[119] In this passage, Jesus attacks their adherence to the traditions of the elders (namely, hand washing) by showing how some of their traditions can be contrary to Jewish law. A son could declare something to be "korban", which made it sacred and a gift to God, something to which no one else could then lay a claim. What was being declared sacred could then be used in any way the owner saw fit, and so was merely a technicality by which sons could avoid their obligations to their parents.

[120] Isa. 29:13

[121] I somewhat elongated the image of a blind guide.

[122] This is another minor addition of mine. The Nile River flows north, which is why southern Egypt was known as "Upper Egypt" and northern Egypt was "Lower Egypt".

[123] Despite this line, the Gospels also say Jesus did not come to get rid of even one iota of the Law. This seeming discrepancy led to the Council of Jerusalem, at which Christians decided kosher laws and circumcision did not need to be followed by Christians.

[124] I found this the most difficult passage to do, thematically, because Jesus seems to be racist against gentiles in it. Therefore, I added the four lines starting with "With boldness matched by your humility…" Since a rejection of gentiles would be so contrary to so much of the

Gospels, I took the message of this passage to be about her initial boldness in approaching Jesus (which would greatly go against accepted rules of behavior in their society) and the tremendous humility she shows in only asking for the scraps that fall from the table.

[125] This line is an allusion to the U2 song, "Mysterious Ways": "If you wanna kiss the sky, better learn how to kneel."

[126] "Ephphatha" is an Aramaic word for "Be opened."

[127] This question is added to the original.

[128] A denarius is the equivalent of the daily wage for a laborer, while a talent is worth 6,000-10,000 denarii. If we estimate that a day's wages

was equal to only $50, then the servant owes the king 3-5 billion dollars! The servant would then be owed about 5 thousand dollars from his fellow servant. If $100/day seems more reasonable, then make it 6-10 billion and 10 thousand, respectively.

I think this story well illustrates how my looser translation in verse can, at times, be more accurate than standard prose translation. Jesus talks about forgiving, not seven times, but seventy times seven times. The point is then illustrated by a king forgiving a man several billion dollars, while this man will not then forgive his fellow servant a few thousand dollars. This point is completely lost when translations say that the servant is owed "a few dollars" (New International Version), "ten dollars" (The Message), "twenty dollars" (Amplified Bible), "an hundred pence" (Wycliffe New Testament, King James Bible, and 21st Century King James Version), "very little money" (New Life Version), or "a hundred shillings" (American Standard Version). A translation like "a few dollars" shows how petty we are in holding grudges over minor offences. If it is several thousand, it urges us to be exceedingly forgiving.

[129] The text does not say what caused the debt. As it was in the billions, I imagined it to be an unbelievable gambling debt, or something like that.

[130] Different ancient manuscripts have this number as 70 or 72, either of which could represent several things. Seventy could represent the elders in Ex. and Num., the number of members of the Sanhedrin, or the number of nations of the earth. Seventy-two could stand for the people in a local council, the princes and kings of the world, the translators of the Greek Old Testament, or the number of nations of the earth (as mistranslated in the Greek Old Testament). Since scholars cannot decide which is more likely, I honestly just chose the one I could rhyme.

[131] The linking of the two as being intertwined is not found in this passage, but is borrowed from the final judgment in Mt. 25, where Jesus says, "In so far as you did this to one of the least of these brothers of Mine, you did it to Me." (Mt. 25:40)

[132] Christ's use of a priest and a Levite (a member of a priestly class) was not meant to illustrate a hypocritical religious class. It was, rather, in response to the lawyer's question about what would lead to eternal life, meant to show the ridiculousness of those who would rather follow laws about ritual purification and "cleanliness" than laws of charity.

[133] This passage is often poorly explained as the false dichotomy of prayer vs. action, while they complement each other in reality. What this passage is really about is women's education. Mary took the role of a student, something that was not permissible for women at that time. Martha, in asking for help, was taking away Mary's chance at an education. It is interesting to think how few ancient culture, or even pre-Industrial Revolution cultures, ever thought women could be educated, despite Jesus standing up for it 2,000 years ago.

[134] The analogy of building something on sand comes from the end of the Sermon on the Mount (Mt. 7:26-27).

[135] This simile is an addition.

[136] The line "You're as much evil..." and the reference to "blasphemy, and bile" are added to the original.

[137] The "queen of the South" is the queen of Sheba, whose story is told in 1 Kings 10: 1-13.

[138] I added the word *alone* to this passage because it struck me that the rich fool was not only talking to himself, but planning what he would be able to say to himself in the future. While I was writing this passage, I read an article in New York Newsday I thought very relevant. A Palestinian man had sent $150,000 home, while he was living in America, in order to build a large enough home for his extended family, a home that was subsequently destroyed by the Israeli army. The Palestinian man said that, while the American dream is to send your kids away to college and live without them, the Palestinian dream is to live with and break your daily bread with your extended family.

[139] While I have mostly avoided allusions to things after the time of Christ, I found this reference to Barry McGuire's "Eve of Destruction" too fitting to pass up.

[140] It seems that Jesus perceived this message was sent by Herod, in order to avoid a confrontation.

[141] The original is not specific in what type of debauchery is referred to, although his brother later refers to "loose women". I included gambling in this group, as it fits the lifestyle.

[142] The analogy of his income to grapes and a vine is added.

[143] "Garçon" is French for "boy," "waiter," or, in this case, "servant."

[144] The steward is not being commended for dishonesty. As steward, he is justly entitled to a percentage of the debt owed to his master. By foregoing his commission on the loans, he is attempting to win himself friends who may hire him in their own dealings.

[145] In a chapter filled with warnings about wealth (Lk. 16), he throws in this tiny passage about divorce. I linked them, but there is no explicit link in the original text.

[146] The blessings and woes found here are from the Sermon on the Plain in Luke's gospel. I combined this speech with Matthew's Sermon on the Mount but could not see leaving one set of beatitudes out or placing them together.

[147] The detail about the vacation is added.

[148] "Mea culpa" is a Latin phrase used to accept guilt, meaning "my fault." In Catholic Mass, many still gently strike their chests when saying this part of the prayer, "I confess to Almighty God and to you my brothers and sisters, that I have sinned through my own fault..."

[149] This would be the "Feast of Booths", or Sukkot, although to what degree the current ceremonial practices reflect those of the first century is speculative.

[150] Most scholars believe the persecution of Christians by Jewish leaders did not begin until after Jesus' death, so these passages in John are most likely referring to the situation at the time the Gospel was written, rather than what happened historically, during Jesus' life on Earth.

[433]

[151] The seventh day of the week was the Sabbath day. A boy was circumcised on his eighth day alive, whether that fell on the Sabbath day or not.

[152] It was commonly believed that, although the Christ would be born in Bethlehem, he would remain hidden someplace until his coming, possibly in heaven. Jesus' heavenly origins prove this tradition.

[153] This quote is based on Is. 44:3.

[154] Nicodemus has such a great story, where he will only meet Jesus at night, in Ch. 3, which seems to be out of fear. By this chapter, he gives Jesus a half-defense, based on the idea that all accused deserve a trial. By the end, he is one of the two people there to bury Jesus.

[155] Although this very famous story is officially in the canon, as part of John's Gospel, it does not exist in many of the oldest and most reliable manuscripts. Based on the style and vocabulary, many think it looks more like something written by the author of Luke's Gospel and Acts, although these things are un-provable.

[156] The text only says that "you will look for Me and you will die in your sin." The comparison to men looking west is my own.

[157] The comparison between Jesus' death and the sun setting, as well as the link between the man gaining his sight back and his sun rising, are additions to the original.

[158] I also added the incident of the blind man falling into the pool earlier, showing people he truly had been blind. The original only has a basic disagreement among the crowd over whether or not this was the blind man.

[159] The vast majority of scholars reject the historicity of Jewish leaders not allowing followers of Jesus to worship in the synagogues. They believe this happened decades after Jesus' death, though John placed this into the story of the life of Jesus, in order to urge his people not to be cowardly, as some Christians were.

[160] This chapter originally began with a passage entitled "Departure to Judea," which read "Once Christ had said these things, He went away,/While people followed, wishing He would stay,/From Galilee into Judea, where/He taught and healed them with the greatest care.", based on Mt. 19:1-2 and Mk. 10:1. I had to remove this when I realized it followed passages from John, in which Jesus is already in Jerusalem, the heart of Judea.

[161] Although I often had a few to choose between a few different rhymes, my most difficult decision was choosing between the above couplet and "They are one flesh, as one roof they live under./What God has joined no man should tear asunder." Although I preferred this rhyme, I used my wife's preference in the passage. In terms of the original text, both the heart and the roof metaphors are additions.

[162] It should be noted that, although this text has been used to support celibacy, the disciples were asking specifically about remarriage.

[163] One of the earliest Christian writers, known as Pseudo-Origen, retold this story and followed the rich young man's claim to have observed the commands with "How do you say 'I have kept the Law and the Prophets'? For it is written in the Law: 'You shall love your neighbors as yourself.' Yet many of your brethren, sons of Abraham, are clothed in filth, dying of hunger, but your house is full of good things, and none of it goes out to them." This is, of course, not recorded in any of the gospels, but I think it gives a great insight into how this issue was originally viewed. It should also be noted that "Do not defraud" is in the original gospels, though not in the Ten Commandments. A famous saying in the early church was "A rich man is either a thief or the son of a thief."

[164] Mephistopheles is one of the highest ranking demons in Christian mythology, but he does not appear in the Bible. He first appears in the Faust legend.

[165] Before people use this passage to claim the rich will have no problem reaching heaven, it should be noted that a thing being "possible with God" is only used in the Gospels in the context of a virgin conceiving a child (Lk. 1:37), faith moving mountains (Mt. 17:20), and curing a possessed boy who was foaming at the mouth (Mk. 9:14-29). One should not bet their salvation on so grand a miracle.

[166] The passages alluded to from the Old Testament (Ps. 82:6, Dt. 1:17, 19:17) link judges to God because judgment is God's.

[167] For those who like to say that John is anti-Semitic, because "the Jews" is often used negatively in his gospel, they should look closely at this passage. Many of "the Jews" came to show their sympathy to Mary and Martha and the plot to kill Jesus came about because so many of "the Jews" believed in Him. Also, often when "the Jews" is used negatively the context refers to the leaders of the Jews.

[168] Much is written about the negative way "the Jews" is used in John's Gospel. It should be noted that (a) the term can refer to Judeans, or the religious leaders of Jews, (b) Christians were seen as a type of Jew early on, and different types of Jews had traditionally written very harshly about other groups, and (c) one cannot judge 2,000 year old texts and imagine Hitler-like anti-Semitism was in the mind of the author, or that he is to blame for all such future bigotry.

[169] For all the attention the negative uses of "the Jews" in John's Gospel gets, it should be noted that Jesus is killed, according to John, because the Lazarus miracle makes too many of "the Jews" believe in Him.

[170] The expectation of a Messiah was not of a divine Son of God, who was king of heaven and Earth, but an earthly king, who would destroy any foreign occupying army and establish a Jewish empire. One can hardly understand why Jesus is killed without understanding the political and social implications of that.

[171] This line about the dead doing nothing but decomposing is an addition.

[172] Jesus came preaching "Love your enemies!", a message they rejected as much as they rejected Him. A generation after Jesus' death, they attempt a revolution against Rome, and failed miserably, with the Temple destroyed, a million people killed, and countless others displaced.

[173] This action of Jesus' might seem incredibly bizarre, but the fig tree was seen as symbolic of the nation of Israel, a symbolism used by many of the prophets, including passages in which Israel faces judgment: Jer. 8:13, 29:17, Hos. 9:10, Joel 1:7, Micah 7:1-6, Hos. 2:12, Is. 3:4.

[174] This occurs in the beginning of John's Gospel, but near the end of the other three. It is worth noting that, in John, this is the first of three Passovers, which is where we get the three year ministry tradition from.

[175] Isaiah 56:7.

[176] All adherents of Judaism in the Roman Empire were required to give one day's wage each year to the Temple in Jerusalem. (Members from each community would go on pilgrimage to Jerusalem to bring this money.) The Temple tax was supposed to be used for the upkeep of the Temple, as well as for works of charity. Jesus is here accusing the Sadducees of corruptly using the money for their own ends. While

in John's gospel, bringing Lazarus back from the dead was the final straw that caused Jesus' death, the cleansing of the Temple was the final straw in the Synoptics.

[177] Psalms 8:2.

[178] Reconstruction of the Temple began in 19 BC, which would place this event at 28 AD. In John's gospel, which gives us this historical detail, the cleansing of the Temple does not happen immediately before Jesus' death, but at least two years before it.

[179] Many have wondered about this part of the story, which is absent from Luke (Lk. 14:15-24), since the man had no invitation in advance to dress for a wedding. Several sources I have read interpret the wedding garment as good deeds, symbolizing someone who accepts the faith in word but does not have the good deeds needed to accompany it.

[180] Jesus asks for a coin to point out their hypocrisy: Jews were not allowed to carry a Roman coin, because it had the image of Caesar on it (Caesar was worshipped as a god, which made this an idolatrous pagan image). The meaning of "Render unto Caesar what is Caesar's" is not a call for any degree of duty to civil authorities, but a call to follow God's law. As Dorothy Day said, "Once you give to God what belongs to God, there is nothing left for Caesar!"

[181] While Matthew and Mark both tell this passage and the one before it, Mark ends the Great Commandment with the line that no one would then challenge him, while Matthew has this line at the end of the question about David's Son. I included it in both.

[182] The headbands and tassels contained the most important words of the Law, which were to be worn as prescribed by Dt. 6:4,8. These were made broad and long as a type of status symbol at the time of Jesus.

[183] This most likely refers to the murder detailed in 2 Ch 24:20-22.

[184] Psalm 118:26

[185] When looking at the eschatological stuff (where it looks like Jesus is predicting the end of the world), one should know that much of it greatly resembles the Fall of Jerusalem, when Rome destroyed the Temple, killed a million people, etc. Too often people take it literally, especially thinking every earthquake, flood, etc., means the world will end.

[186] On the one hand, this line, and the one a few pages later about this all happening before this generation passes, obviously did not come true, literally, and could makes Jesus look like his prophecy was completely wrong. But these Gospels were written down 30-60 years after Jesus' death, at which point it obviously had not come true.

[187] This metaphor, which is in the Gospel, is just to illustrate that the appearance of one thing (vultures) can indicate another (a corpse).

[188] The incident of the third servant misplacing the money and finding it is my own addition.

[189] This 21-line response of Jesus is an expansion of the simple response 'Truly I say to you, to the extent that you did not do it to one of the least of these, you did not do it to Me.' (Mt. 25:45) I made a rare exception in taking this liberty because so many people are starving in this world while so many live in excess. I thought, since this passage has been so greatly ignored, its message must be shouted from the rooftops, so in my work adding passion to it was the best I could do.

[190] Isaiah 53:1

[191] Isaiah 6:10

[192] As mentioned earlier (in "Jesus Heals the Man Born Blind"), most historians doubt that followers of Christ were banned from synagogues and the Temple during Jesus' life, but that this was a later event John moves into the story to urge his readers to be courageous.

[193] Psalms 41:9.

[194] The reference to the setting sun is an addition.

[195] Zechariah 13:7.

[196] This couplet is an addition. The second line is from Yeats' poem, "No Second Troy", which seemed incredibly relevant to this passage, even though the poem itself is unrelated.

[197] The instruction to buy a sword should not be seen as a reversal of Jesus' teaching against violence. Many people in this society carried a sword, mainly for protection from wild animals.

[198] The reference to a womb is an addition.

[199] The comparison to men gaining children is also an addition.

[200] The reference to light is added as well.

[201] This metaphor, which repeats the theme of the lines before it, is an addition taken from an Irish saying.

[202] The reference to a plant without water and light is an addition.

[203] I expanded "much fruit" into an analogy of seeds that grow an entire forest. Also, I left out a line about those who abide in Jesus' words receiving from God what they ask for, although that idea has appeared in earlier passages.

[204] The chain simile, as well as the images of hugging and Jesus' fold are all additions.

[205] The original line is "but because you are not of the world, but I chose you out of the world, therefore the world hates you." (RSV) Also, while Jesus warns they will be hated because of their separation from the world, I added, in the next two lines, it being proportional.

[206] Jesus referring to His persecution as appearing like a disastrous defeat is added, as well as the vine metaphor.

[207] This line about a noose is entirely added.

[208] Psalms 35:19 and 69:4.

[209] The fire symbolism is an addition.

[210] The sons of Zebedee are James and John.

[211] The people fall back because Jesus' use of "I AM", if He were not the Son of God, would be incredibly blasphemous. (In Ex. 3:14, God identifies Himself to Moses as "I AM WHO I AM.")

[212] The detail about Christ being punched is an addition.

[213] Acts 1:15-20 tells a different, significantly more graphic story about how Judas died. Since my book is based on the Gospels, primarily, I used Matthew's version.

[214] Zechariah 11:12-13.

[215] The text merely says that Barabbas committed murder, but does not say how this was done.

[216] That Pilate made this statement to ridicule the crowd, and because he could not deal with the tension of it, is my own addition and interpretation of the event.

[217] Recently, the possible inclusion of this statement from the Gospels in Mel Gibson's "The Passion of the Christ" caused a great deal of controversy, since it has been cited as justification for anti-Semitism. If one reads John 9, it seems apparent that many Jews thought guilt could be inherited, though Jesus did not, so this statement could very well be historical. And, since I do not accept the idea that Jews inherit the guilt of the crucifixion, nor do I accept guilt for anti-Semitic acts done by Christians in the past. Therefore, I see no reason to change our Gospel for the sins of some long-deceased Christians.

[218] This line is my addition, just to point out the ridiculousness of preserving His life so that He can live long enough to be nailed to a cross.

[219] Psalms 22:18.

[220] The image of God's hand covering the light is an addition.

[221] Jesus has not lost faith in His Father, as this saying may appear to suggest. This line is the first line of Psalm 22, which describes someone who suffers much as Jesus had suffered and yet, in the end, still glorifies God.

[222] The medical explanation of why the legs were broken, so people suffocated, is added.

[223] Many have viewed the water and blood as symbolic of the Eucharist and Baptism, though I have also heard this forms under the heart when someone has a heart attack.

[224] Exodus 12:46, Psalms 34:20.

[225] Zechariah 12:10.

[226] The Resurrection was the most difficult passage in terms of combining the Gospels, because all four Gospels tell the story, but with very different details. I tried to use as much from all four as possible, and add a degree of excitement, shock, and confusion, such that one could imagine four different stories emerging from this one event. The most significant difference is that I have Mary Magdalene arrive with a group of women, as the Synoptic Gospels tell us, but at the confusion of the empty tomb, she separates from the rest, in order to set up the scene from John's Gospel.

Here is a brief outline of some of the details and how the Gospels differ:
Mt: Mary Magdalene and the other Mary, earthquake, one angel rolled back stone, guards became like dead men, angel tells them not to be afraid, that Jesus has risen, that they must tell this to His disciples, and that Christ would meet them in Galilee.
Mk: Mary Magdalene, Mary the mother of James, and Salome, brought spices, stone was already rolled back, met a young man in a white robe who tells them not to be amazed, that Jesus has risen, that they must tell this to His disciples, and that Christ would meet them in Galilee.
Lk: "The women who had come with Him from Galilee", brought spices, found stone rolled away, but no body, two men in dazzling clothing appear, they bow to the ground in fear, asked why they seek the living among the dead, reminded that Jesus foretold His resurrection, and they relay this to the other disciples.
Jn: Mary Magdalene arrives by herself and, seeing the stone had been moved, runs to Peter and the beloved disciple to tell them Jesus' body was taken away; Peter and the beloved disciple run to the tomb, the beloved disciple arrives first but lets Peter enter before him, they leave after seeing the empty tomb, Mary Magdalene remains outside the tomb, weeping, while two angels ask the reason for her tears, Mary sees Jesus but does not recognize Him, He also asks why she is crying, thinking He was the gardener, she asks where Jesus' body was placed, He calls her name, she calls Him "Rabboni!", Mary is told to give witness of this to the brethren.

[227] Since I had the women arrive at an empty tomb and then be greeted by the two angels (as is the case in Luke), I felt the need to change the cause of the guards falling unconscious from seeing the angels (Mt. 28:4) to the earthquake.

[228] The line about replacing sorrow with hope is an addition.

[229] Although Jesus and the angels ask women to give witness to the resurrection, Peter and the beloved disciple needed to verify what Mary said was true because women could not legally be witnesses in their society.

[230] The dialogue in Luke's Gospel is attributed to the two travelers, but not divided into two parts, as I have done.

[231] This statement of the obvious, that Jesus could not have survived crucifixion, is an addition. Although the claim that He survived it is made often enough, this is historically moronic. The Romans knew how to kill people and, barring a miracle as fantastic as Resurrection, no one could survive an execution.

[232] This line, as well as the two before it, are an addition. I used this opportunity to explain to those not familiar with Jewish concept of the Messiah that most expected a political savior, who would overthrow Roman occupation and establish an earthly political kingdom

[233] The number 153 is significant because that is how many known species of fish there were at the time of Jesus.

[234] This line is an addition. In Matthew and Mark, the disciples are told to meet Him in Galilee, whereas Luke has them meet Jesus in Jerusalem. I needed to add this line to bring them to the following scene, in Jerusalem.

[235] Both references to the sun and light, four lines later, are additions.

[236] Joel 3:1-5.

[237] Psalms 16:8-11.

[238] Psalms 110:1.

About the Author and Illustrator

Joseph Muller was born on May 9, 1980, growing up in the East Flatbush section of Brooklyn, NY. He went to Cathedral Prep Seminary, in the Elmhurst area of Queens, NY, where he and Sean met. At Fordham University, he met Jennifer Reardon, whom he married and has had two children with, Sean and Keira. In 2006, he received his M.A. in Biblical Theology from St. John's University and has since taught there as an adjunct professor, while also teaching theology on the high school level.

Sean V Cleary is an illustrator who works mainly with traditional pen and ink. He lives in New York City with his wife and two children.

Made in the USA
Middletown, DE
24 August 2019